CONTEMPORARY JAPANESE CERAMICS

FIRED with PASSION

CONTEMPORARY
JAPANESE CERAMICS

FIRED with
PASSION

SAMUEL J. LURIE and BEATRICE L. CH

Principal photography by Geoff Spear

Design by Lurie, Chang and Spear

Eagle Art Publishing, Inc.
New York

Dedicated to Gabrielle W. Lurie

First edition, 2006

Printed in China

ISBN: 1-891640-38-0

Library of Congress Cataloging-in-Publication data available

Jacket and Front Matter Illustrations

Jacket front: Tsuboi Asuka. *Girl Sending a Message*, 2003. H. 28 1/2 in. x w. 25 1/4 in. x d. 25 1/4 in. (71 cm x 63 cm x 63 cm). See p. 59, fig. 59

Jacket back: Tokuda Yasokichi. Plates, overglaze enamels, 1999. Diam. 29 1/2 in. (74.9 cm). See p. 215, fig. 172

P. ii: Hinoda Takashi. *Untitled*. See p. 61, fig. 67

P. iii: Hayashi Yasuo. *Work 69-B*. See p. 31, fig. 26

Pp. vi, vii: Isheguro Munemaro. Jar, with detail. See p. 58, fig. 48

P. x: Nakashimi Harumi. See p. 167

P. xi: Clay figurine (Dogu), Final Jomon, 1500–500 BC. See p. 22

P. xiii: Shibata Masamitsu. *Plate*, 2002. H. 2 in. x w. 6.5 in. (5.08 cm x 16.5 cm)

P. xiv, top: Wakao Toshisada. *Leaf-shaped side dish*. H. 2 in x l. 7 in. (5.08 cm x 17.8 cm)

p. xiv, bottom: Nakamura, Takuo. *Rectangular plate*. H. 1.7 in. x l. 10 in. (4.3 cm x 25 cm)

P. xv, top: Kato Tsubusa. *Round dish*. H. 3.5 in. x w. 8 in. (8.9 cm x 20.32 cm)

P. xv, bottom: Higashida Shigemasa. *Oribe side dish*. H. 1 in. x l. 8 in. (2.54 cm x 20.32 cm)

P. xvi: Kaneshige Kosuke. *Birth of Kings*, 1991. See p. 112

P. xvii: Kaneshige Toyo. *Bizen tea bowl* (c. 1960s). See p. 232, fig. 184

Contents

Acknowledgments

This book could not have been written without the contributions of three remarkable women. My wife, Gabrielle, to whom this book is dedicated, was my equal partner in every respect when we first encountered Japanese ceramics many years ago, and she has continued to fully participate in our exploration of the artistry of Japanese ceramics. Her discerning eye and good judgment must be credited for much of the success we have had. On a personal level, her remarkable character, steady support and infinite patience have been more than any wife should be required to possess.

I cannot give enough praise to my co-author, Beatrice L. Chang. Anyone who has been lucky enough to meet her knows that she has great knowledge of Japanese ceramics, which she conveys with an infectious warmth and enthusiasm. Over the years her love for this material has grown to embrace the work of less familiar but more interesting and adventurous contemporary Japanese ceramists. Her work ethic, zest, kindness to all—clients, artists and this collaborator—is nothing short of amazing.

I must risk embarrassing my extraordinary, but modest, office manager, Felicia Janetti. For more decades than she would feel comfortable about discussing, she has been the source of wisdom and understanding coupled with the highest office skills. She has not only earned our trust and affection, but has given enormous help in getting this book through its many drafts.

SJL

It is a pleasure to thank J. Edward ("Ted") Kidder, Jr., who has long been recognized as a pre-eminent authority on early Japanese pottery. He wears his learning lightly and he has given valuable encouragement to our project to make Japanese ceramics better known and appreciated by the general art-loving public. Lastly, we wish to thank Marta Kalicka for her meticulous assistance.

SJL and BLC

Preface

I consider myself to be unusually fortunate. It is a great gift in life to be the director of an art gallery, an occupation so meaningful and so pleasurable. At Dai Ichi Arts Gallery, I am surrounded by beautiful and compelling art objects and by the passionate, quirky, intellectual and generous people who make them and collect them. From tea bowls and vessels to avant-garde sculpture, the objects that populate my gallery retain the intention and spirit of their makers, which seem almost to animate them. Carried away with enthusiasm for a vase or sculpture, I catch myself talking to them: "What kind of flower do you want to hold?" "Tell me your story— where do you fit in Japan's ceramic tradition?" Sumptuous catalogues and books about historical and contemporary ceramics may excite me so much that sometimes I cannot fall asleep at night. Receiving superb pieces at the gallery is like receiving Christmas gifts throughout the year. When one of my artists has really stretched himself or herself, or had a breakthrough idea or technique, I celebrate with them and honor their quest for their fullest artistic expression. My mission is to scour Japan for the very best contemporary ceramic art and to share this bounty with increasing numbers of passionate collectors, both private individuals and institutions.

From the moment of first contact in the 16th century, the West has fallen in love with Japanese art again and again. Enthusiasm for *Japonisme* captivated James McNeill Whistler, Vincent Van Gogh, and other notable painters. Frank Lloyd Wright gathered a distinguished collection of Japanese woodblock prints. The Japanese potter Shoji Hamada (1894-1978) came frequently to the United States and influenced generations of potters and artists. In architecture, fashion and design, the influence of Japanese art and aesthetics is apparent in various aspects of minimalism, love of nature and natural materials, and, more recently, *anime* (animated films) and *manga* (cartoon-like books for adult readers). The East-West dialogue has been facilitated by the internet, ease of travel, and other modern advances. Today, Japanese ceramic artists participate in the full spectrum of artistic trends, both traditional and cutting-edge.

Collectors of Japanese ceramics now have more resources at their disposal than ever before, but still many important books and catalogues are available only in Japanese. Museum exhibitions from time to time highlight contemporary Japanese ceramics, although they still tend to favor antique objects (essential viewing if one wants to fully appreciate contemporary artists). My co-author, Samuel J. Lurie, and I thought the time was ripe for a new sort of book on Japanese ceramics that would focus on seeing and appreciating contemporary ceramics. In this book we lead you on a guided tour of some of the best Japanese ceramics from pre-history to the present day. In simple, everyday language we discuss some of the key periods, issues and trends in Japanese history that continue to engage both Japanese and Western potters today: the Jomon and Momoyama eras, the seemingly never-ending dispute about the value of "art" versus "craft", the influence of Tea Ceremony. Experts have written thick volumes about each of these factors; here we strip them to their bare essentials in order to lay a foundation for the appreciation of contemporary movements and styles. Our chief concern is to introduce the reader to outstanding examples of contemporary Japanese ceramics and explain what we see in each—specifically, how they astonish, captivate and enlighten us. Using our responses as a guide and point of departure, we hope each reader will undertake their own journey of investigation and appreciation. A world of pleasure awaits!

In writing this book with Sam, I have been tested, questioned, and challenged on many different levels beyond aesthetic appreciation. Emotion and artistic discernment still play a crucial role, but now the intellect must take over. How can the material be best organized? How can we best communicate to others what we know about Japanese ceramics and help it all make sense? The challenge made me read more widely, think more deeply, and explore more aggressively.

Sam was the inspiration for this book. He is a collector and a very serious one. He loves the objects; he cannot part with them. He protects them, he talks about them, and he can be possessive, jealous, like a lover. He is the ideal writing partner—intelligent, informed, passionate, persuasive, nitpicking, maddening. A perfectionist, he insisted that we review virtually all published ceramic art books, interview many photographers before hiring Geoff, and revise the text again and again. Each revision was undertaken to make the book more comprehensive, more compelling, more understandable, and more up to the minute.

Sam and I are the grateful recipients of much help, advice and love during the writing of this book. They say behind every great man, there is a great woman. The woman behind Sam is his dear wife, Gabrielle. I believe she has been the first, and will be the last, reader of this book before printing. It has also been her labor of love.

Dai Ichi Arts, Ltd. started with Jerry Oppenheim, Natalie Fitz-Gerald, John Guth and Kenneth W. Jiang. They planted the seed and they were the wind under my wings. Their vision, their faith, and their support were indispensable. I am lucky to have Patricia Pelehach as my dear friend. She is always supportive, always there to listen, share, and to laugh. And I must thank my daughter, Christine S. Jiang, whom I love dearly and cherish and who prevents me from taking myself too seriously. I hope that when she too finds her life's work in this wonderful land, she will discover that it is also her life's pleasure and passion.

To all who love superb art, I hope you enjoy this book and find it both stimulating and useful. May it widen your knowledge and deepen your appreciation of Japanese ceramics.

B.L.C

Introduction

The ambitious purpose of this book is to introduce you to—no, really, to captivate you with—a new world of stunning art that is barely known in the West: contemporary Japanese ceramics.

Japanese ceramics originated some 15,000 years ago (or 16,000 years ago, based on 1999 radiocarbon tests) and are the oldest known in the world, older than the oldest Chinese ceramics discovered thus far, far older than Egyptian, Near Eastern and Greek pottery.[1] During Japan's unequaled ceramic history, its potters developed uniquely beautiful, sometimes profoundly beautiful, pottery that exists nowhere else, culminating in the work produced since 1945. Although considerations of its long history may add a certain charm, that does not begin to account for the enthusiasm we have brought to this publication. Quite simply, it is to make better known the singular aesthetic achievements of today's Japanese ceramic artists that provides our motivation for publishing.

What should be said that would provide useful guidance? Merely calling a piece "beautiful" but not going any further, would not be helpful. A good solution is provided by Bernard Berenson, the celebrated art connoisseur, in his book *Italian Painters of the Renaissance*. In his preface, he wrote that his book:

"...does not attempt to give an account of the painters' domestic lives or even of specific techniques, but of what their pictures mean to us today as works of art, of what they can do for us as ever contemporary life-enhancing actualities. The text may help the reader to understand what the reproductions tell him, and may make him ask what he feels when he looks at them and try to account for his reactions while enjoying a work of visual art..."

We have tried to convey in some detail why we love these pieces by offering specific explanations which target the telling detail or give insights thought to be important. While scholarly information and references are absent, enough background facts and context have been provided

---

[1] Tatsuo Kobayashi, *Jomon Reflections*, Oxbow Books 2004, pp. 19, 30, fn. 1 at p. 190.

to enable the reader to start his own fulfilling aesthetic journey. Both the text and the comments on the illustrations focus on what these ceramics "mean to us today as works of art," and the enjoyment they can provide as "contemporary life-enhancing actualities"; to stimulate the reader to examine what "he feels when he looks at the illustrations." The stress is on aesthetic enjoyment, the ineffable pleasure that works of art can provide. The Further Reading section lists sources for more complete information.

Although this book is about ceramics after 1945, we have included a brief history of Japanese ceramics in the next section. Completely ignoring this rich history, providing no clue to the remarkable achievements of the past, was unacceptable. That basic information will also enable the reader to begin to understand how a great deal of today's work has fruitfully evolved out of Japan's centuries-old, even millennia-old, ceramic traditions and will, hopefully, whet the reader's interest to further investigate.

The selections reflect our personal aesthetic taste in

choosing what we regard as being among the finest works. Of course, aesthetic judgments invite controversy. The omission of some favorite artists or styles cannot, will not and should not pass without criticism. Informed passionate opinion is a healthy characteristic of the committed art lover whose juices run hot, pro or con, when encountering living art, whether ancient or contemporary.

Our inclusion of some lesser known artists is another matter entirely. They may be seen to fit uncomfortably with greater ceramic artists. However, they are not shown for lifetime achievement but only because an individual work of theirs is, in our opinion, outstanding. A modest reputation does not mean that all work will be mediocre. In the opposite situation, too often a great name attached to inferior work has led over-awed critics to exaggerate its worth.

We have selected works of art, not brand names. We have not offered a parade of the best known ceramists, although many are included, nor have we been restricted to the most important artists, as judged by experts. Speaking plainly, our overriding criterion has been our independent evaluation of the aesthetic quality of individual ceramic works.

We anticipate that many will share our taste and be led into this marvelous new world. Japanese ceramics are a vibrant art form. The banquet of exciting contemporary work, still mostly affordably priced, should encourage wider support for these artists. An interesting aside: what reactions will the Japanese have to the views of passionate foreigners about their great ceramic art?

It bears repetition to state that neither the selection of the artists, the specific works, nor our comments are intended to be anything more than an expression of our considered opinions. We do not pretend to have said the last word on any of these subjects. It is our wish that this survey will stimulate the reader's independent imaginative exploration.

Special Pleasures of Ceramics

Arguably, better than other sculptural media, clay offers boundless shaping and painting opportunities, limited only by the artist's imagination. It is more malleable than metal, wood or glass; it can avoid the cold feel of metal and glass. The variety of clay surfaces offers an unsurpassed range of tactile and visual feasts. Finally, fired clay has a truly surprising ability to survive indefinitely in good condition, even after being buried for thousands of years.

Almost no one has ever physically handled the surface of a painting by Rembrandt or Picasso. Apart from the resulting damage, that would be pointless since it would add nothing to our understanding or pleasure. Ceramics are entirely different in this respect. Like the human body, ceramics can be brought to a new life by appropriate touching, by appropriate handling. Sometimes its silky surface should be lightly caressed or held in both hands to better feel and understand its forms and weight; at other times its rough surface should be gingerly explored. Superior ceramics, especially Japanese, commonly offer what is best described as a sensual physical pleasure, a quality Western critical literature rarely mentions, nor does that literature discuss that touching brings a deep, primitive awareness, a different, entirely valid, kind of knowledge of a ceramic work. One can sometimes feel the impressions of the potter's fingers in the clay work, which may be centuries old or made by a celebrated artist. This is a wonderful experience, almost paranormal, yet comfortable, that enables one to share the creative process, to almost shake hands in intimate communication with the potter, whether ancient or contemporary, in a uniquely personal way.

The bulk of traditional ceramics are functional, made for practical use. For example, pottery has for centuries been used as flower containers, informally or in formal flower arrangement modes. The flowers then form an integral whole with the ceramic vessel. Enhanced by a creative flower arrangement, an artistic totality may emerge that is greater than its two component parts.

Superb ceramic eating, drinking or serving utensils can elevate that experience above the basic alimentary level. The placement of food on a dish need not be governed solely by practical considerations of providing a surface for efficiently cutting, spearing or scooping food into the mouth. The dish may be recognized as potentially more than a bland presence. Its shape, color, size and surface texture may be sensitively related to the food it holds, utterly enhancing dining (**pages xiii, xiv, xv**).

While this has been understood in many parts of the world, the Japanese have raised the complete art of dining to unmatched heights. At the highest level is the Kaiseki meal, which originally referred to the food service in connection with the tea ceremony, and now is more loosely applied to other specially prepared meals. A well-designed Japanese meal may reject the use of a single "set" of dishes, as is favored in the West. Each utensil may be different in color, size and shape and selections may vary according to the seasons. A small amount of food will be artfully arranged on the dish, allowing the beauty of the dish to be appreciated while serving as a suitable background for the food. The ensemble becomes a true feast for the eyes, encouraging slow consumption for maximum pleasure.

After studying the works illustrated, the reader may recognize that Japanese ceramics may have a distinctive flavor. Although difficult to define and varying from artist to artist, there is a certain solidity or weight, a seriousness of purpose, a love of glaze itself, natural or applied, an unexcelled skill in execution that often marks quality Japanese ceramics. One senses that Japanese ceramists often show an almost mystical respect for the specific qualities of clay, of "clayness," and a sense of privilege of making art in this medium.

Is this related to the fact that Japanese potters, even those working in completely nontraditional modes, are well aware of ancient Japanese ceramics and that they are contemporary practitioners of a long-standing honored art? It would be difficult for today's ceramic artists not to be daily reminded of their historical roots since the essential material, techniques and even the centers of production have changed so little over the centuries. There is even continuity within many families, where professional potters follow their art generation after generation. They are proud to be contributing to this heritage, to which they feel a specific responsibility. The most serious ceramists believe they are engaged in a calling, not a vocation. We are the lucky witnesses to an explosively creative multi-faceted art scene, enhanced by links to a distant past, which we hope to illuminate in the pages that follow.

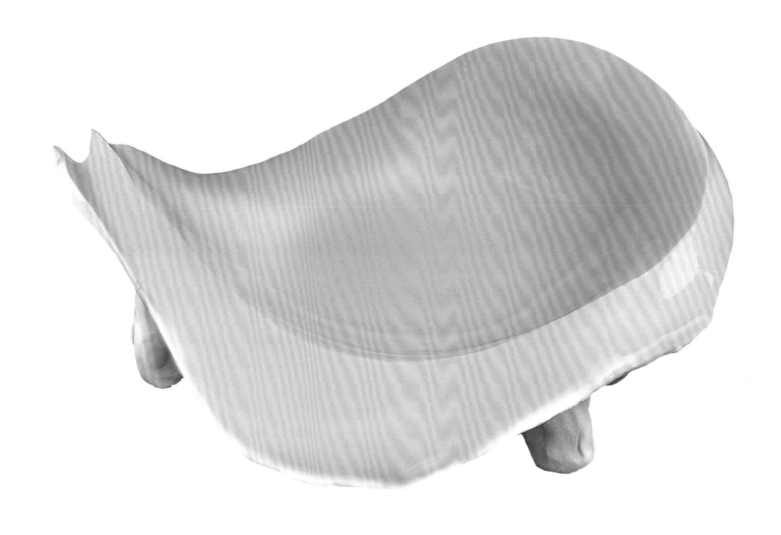

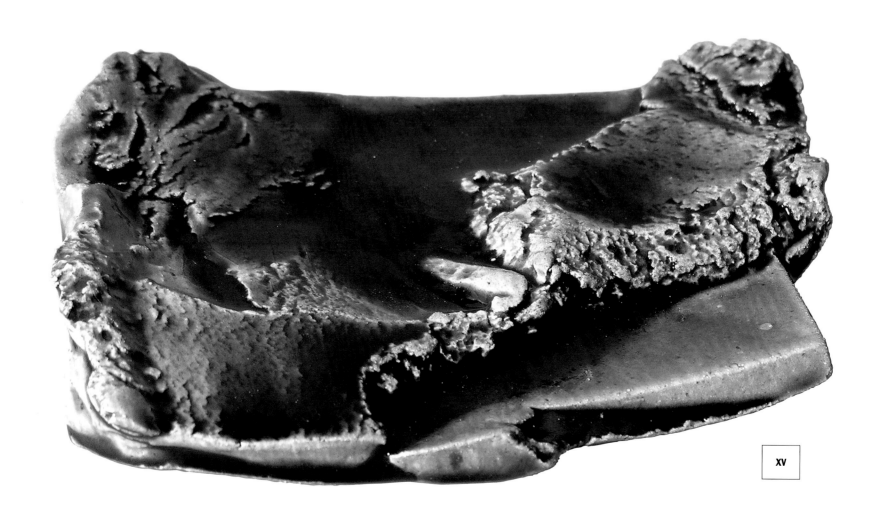

Functional v. Sculptural Ceramics

The process of selecting work for inclusion required us to confront the old quarrel about the relative worth of traditional utilitarian vessels and non-functional sculptural pieces. We question whether any meaningful judgment about aesthetic quality can be made based solely on the distinction between contemporary ceramics that take the form of traditional functional vessels, and contemporary ceramics that largely discard tradition by producing non-functional sculpture. Those hostile to traditional pottery commonly look askance at the utilitarian aspect of its vessels, negatively describing all such work as conservative and repetitive, offering little opportunity for individual expression. Those who prefer non-traditional ceramics use positive language to describe their work as sculptural art, which provides an opportunity for self-expression and originality, not as lowly vessels made for mere use. A further complication is that a vessel today could be described by a linguistically adept artist as being a form with an opening, thus deflecting or, perhaps, avoiding the pejorative category of functional pottery.

We are not convinced that the dogma of art for art's sake, which would tend to favor non-utilitarian ceramics, is any more persuasive than other facile generalities of aesthetic criteria. There is no shame in being useful; there is no virtue in being useless. Each work of either type should be examined solely on the basis of its aesthetic quality, without any preconceptions.

It is true that much traditional pottery is, from our perspective, simply dull, uninspired, merely a duplication of earlier models. Such work, still produced in abundance in Japan to satisfy a large, persistent demand for the comfortably familiar, has a lesser place in our survey of contemporary ceramics. On the other hand, it would

be a serious error if, after recognizing some characteristics of a traditional style, one leaped to the conclusion that the work must be of little merit. If fairly examined, one may discover that old styles, quite often, continue to be invigorated. In all candor, it must be emphasized that the authors' viewpoint is the product of a markedly differ-

ent cultural background. A balanced approach—not our aim—would be mindful of the complex networks of meanings that traditional ceramics have to the Japanese, and give them greater representation. Their involvement with tradition is far deeper and widespread than is shared by Americans. We are comparatively new-born as a nation and as artists. Our association with our brief past does not begin to have a comparable hold on our imagination. A love of change, of the latest in art fashions, characterizes U.S. culture.

The Japanese veneration of tradition is woefully distorted by thinking it is simply a dull, mindless compliance with the past. They may intuitively make connections between their love of traditional ceramics and, for example, with the preservation of the ineffable pleasures of their ubiquitous temples and gardens. But this is not the place to explore the ways in which their long ceramic tradition is bound to countless other desirable elements of their culture. Our selections represent only our preferences for traditional work that is coupled with innovation, and even more to our taste, the excitement of creative ceramic sculpture.

We have not automatically included works merely because they are sculptural, non-functional, and without any discernible traditional references. We have avoided sculpture that possesses zero visual interest and makes only a strained, banal conceptual point.

Art v. Craft

Another old notion that deserves to be buried is the alleged dichotomy of art versus craft, a misleading distinction without a difference. No judicious evaluation of works in clay is possible for those who have the unwarranted prejudice that anything made from clay must be branded by the lower status category of craftwork, not fine art. There is no rational basis for this disdain, for this automatic downgrading. A work is not better or worse aesthetically simply because of its material—stone, clay, wood, metal, whatever. We must be aware of, and disregard, this foolish habit of "thought." As criteria of quality, the art/craft, stone/clay and sculpture/utilitarian distinctions make no aesthetic or theoretical sense. We have endeavored to make our selections free from any of these biases. All ceramic work has the potential for aesthetic excellence or sterility; any style ceramic piece may be, or may not be, an exciting, beautiful, creative artistic work.

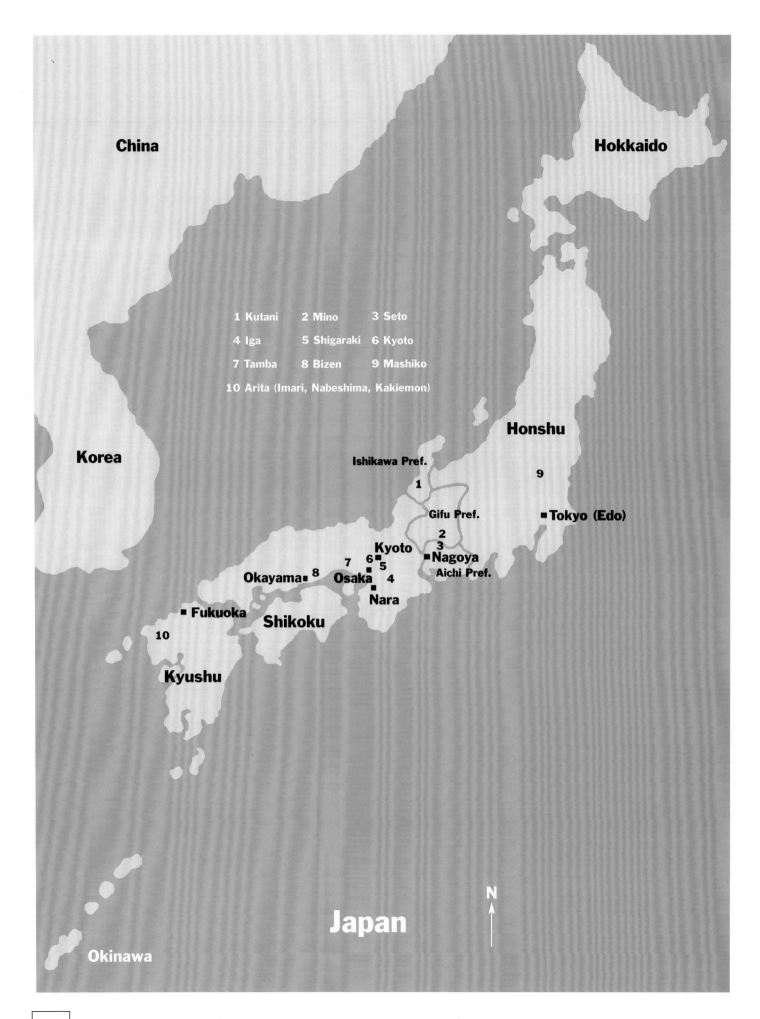

China

Hokkaido

1 Kutani   2 Mino   3 Seto
4 Iga   5 Shigaraki   6 Kyoto
7 Tamba   8 Bizen   9 Mashiko
10 Arita (Imari, Nabeshima, Kakiemon)

Honshu

Korea

Ishikawa Pref.

1

9

Gifu Pref.

Tokyo (Edo)

2
3

Kyoto
6   5
7   4
Okayama   8   Osaka   Nagoya
Nara   Aichi Pref.

Fukuoka

Shikoku

10

Kyushu

N

Japan

Okinawa

The Legacy: A Brief History Until 1945

The archeological record, including the discovery of stone tools with intentionally ground edges on hand-held axes, fully supports the conclusion that the islands of Japan have been inhabited for at least 30,000 years. Immigration from the Asian mainland to Japan is thought to have occurred by both land and sea routes. It is believed that there was a land bridge between Hokkaido, the northernmost island of Japan, and the Asian mainland during the last Ice Age, when sea levels were much lower, and even during the warming period at the end of that Ice Age, some 11,000 years ago. In addition, the narrow strait between Korea and Kyushu, Japan's main southern island, could have been successfully crossed by primitive boats.

Jomon Period (13,000 BC–500 BC)

The oldest pottery ever found in Japan, or in any other place in the world, dated approximately 13,000 BC, is undecorated and known only by small fragments. Its appearance marks the beginning of the period called "Jomon," or "cord mark," referring to a decoration made on pottery by rolling a cord or rope on a soft clay surface before firing. Not all Jomon Period pots have cord decorations, and this decorative technique also occurs in the next period, Yayoi. The very existence of the Jomon culture, as a culture, was not known until 1877 when an American, Edward Sylvester Morse (1838–1925), made the first scientific archeological excavation of Jomon pottery. During the last few decades, *thousands* of Jomon sites have been discovered in all regions of the country. Jomon pottery has been divided into six periods, based on analyses of style, a criterion not relevant to our purposes. For the same reason, not all post-Jomon periods are mentioned in this brief survey.

No kilns have been found for Jomon pottery. Hand-built by the coil method, without the use of a turntable or wheel, Jomon pottery was low-fired, probably made in open bonfires. We know that the Jomon people were essentially hunter-gatherers, who subsisted on animals that they hunted and killed, on plants which grew in the wild, fish that they caught and clams that they collected. By today's standards, the Jomon people were short, with women averaging about four feet eight inches and men five feet two inches. They rarely lived beyond their thirtieth birthday. This was a pre-literate time.

Artistically, the greatest Jomon Period is Middle Jomon (3,500–2,500 BC), which featured complex, gorgeous, sometimes outrageous, "flame-style" rim decorations. The best examples have an unmatched wild exuberance and flamboyance, unique in the world history of pottery (**fig. 1**). Equally compelling are Middle Jomon vessels whose elegant designs are remarkably disciplined (**fig. 2**).

Such pots were obviously not used simply to prepare food. The large quantity of their artistic embellishments negate any intended utilitarian purposes. Top-heavy, flame-style vessels with ornate rim decorations, left no room for efficient pouring or drinking. Massive tops, set upon relatively narrow bodies, resulted in instability, not ideal for storage. Elaborate, brittle patterns appliqued onto the body discouraged casual rough handling. Although one known use for some large Middle Jomon jars was for burying the dead, the elaborate flame-style rim jars were not used for that purpose.

Nothing is actually known about the spiritual life of the Jomon. Undeterred by the lack of evidence, the twin attributes of impracticality and beauty of Middle Jomon vessels have led some learned commentators to conclude that they must have solely had a ritual or religious function. This

FIG. 1. MIDDLE JOMON PERIOD

FIG. 2. MIDDLE JOMON PERIOD

3

conclusion is enlightening only as to the mind of those scholars less interested in matters aesthetic. Such "authorities" assume, without discussion, that there is no possibility that the Jomon people could have created those masterpieces, largely because they craved and recognized beauty. Is this far-fetched? Is it not rare to find a human group anywhere, whether or not they have the word beauty in their vocabulary, that does not exhibit a preference for certain objects, regardless of any extra utility, on the basis of their pleasing appearance? Is there any evidence that the basic nature of the human race has changed over the past 5,000 years? Did the Jomon fail to respond to sunsets, or snow-covered fields, or shimmering lakes? Are we less aggressive and violent than the Jomon people? If forced to speculate, we would include the possibility that these glorious creations made Middle Jomon hearts sing, were expressions of their need for aesthetic nourishment, that beauty was an important value in their lives (**fig 1, 2**).

The remarkable Jomon clay sculptures of the human figure, known as "Dogu", were produced from approximately 7,000 BC through 500 BC, the end of the Jomon Period. The finest of these works are notable for their inventive freedom: sometimes done in abstract style, sometimes employing expressive anatomic deformation or prominent body decorations, almost always emotionally charged and occasionally haunting (**figs. 3, 4, p.xi**). Whatever their original magic, religious, aesthetic, or other usage, they possess the power to excite 21st century art lovers.

It is fascinating to try to deal with what appears to be a Jomon paradox, given our inadequate knowledge. Let us imagine the pre-literate Middle Jomon hunters returning to their crude huts after their days in the forest, killing wildlife with stone weapons and arrows. We find it difficult to understand the incongruity that such primitive people were making sophisticated, imaginative clay works. How can we explain their flair and originality? This is, quite sim-

ply, astounding. Their success upsets a common preconception that only a large "civilized" community, one with ample leisure time, basking in clement weather, abundant food supplies, peace and safety from invasion, can provide the necessary conditions to produce great art.

Yayoi Period (500 BC–250 AD)

The end of the Jomon Period, at the start of the Yayoi Period, c. 500 BC, is marked by the introduction of wet rice field farming, that is, full-scale agriculture. However, recent archeological discoveries have provided some evidence that the Yayoi Period began earlier, in approximately 900 BC. Yayoi is a name derived from the specific shell-mound in Tokyo where this type of low-fired, unglazed pottery was first found in 1884.

Who were the Jomon people and the Yayoi people? Despite the great length of the Jomon Period and extensive archeological investigation, we still know very little about these people. One body of opinion holds that the Jomon were the ancestors of the modern Ainu, who today live in Hokkaido, the cold, northernmost island of Japan; that the Yayoi were immigrants from Korea, the Yamato people, who may have been the ancestors of the present-day Japanese population. It is accepted that the Yayoi averaged about two inches more in height than the Jomon people, and arrived in Japan not only with the superior knowledge of rice farming, but also with the technologies of iron and bronze making. While there is no doubt that substantial immigration occurred from Korea into Japan, there is disagreement regarding the extent, timing, and the significance of that immigration.

However, in our opinion, questions regarding the racial or national composition of Jomon and Yayoi people, and their relationship to the modern Japanese population, is of lesser interest than the remarkable achievements in Japanese ceramic art that resulted.

In contrast with most Jomon pottery, Yayoi pottery is characterized by pure shapes and a controlled, even minimal, approach to decoration. Yayoi pottery has a distinctive classic style. Its simple elegance does not involve the loss of sensuous form, nor a lessening of basic formal strength (**fig. 5**). This Yayoi aesthetic appears to be the origin of a fundamental Japanese artistic preference, in ceramics and some other arts, that has remained unchanged throughout its history. Yayoi style pottery continued to be produced well beyond the 3rd century, the usual date given as the end of the Yayoi Period.

Kofun Period Through Muromachi Period (250–1568)

"Kofun" means old tomb. Keyhole-shaped burial mounds, believed to be characteristic of imperial tombs, first appeared about 250 AD, the date assigned to the beginning of the Kofun Period. The most striking thing about Kofun burial mounds is their colossal size and great number. There are over 10,000 mound tombs in Japan. Many of the mound tombs exceed 200 meters in length; the smallest are 5 meters in length. One emperor's tomb is 485 meters long, 305 meters wide, and 35 meters high. Another is 415 meters long. They both cover a larger ground area than the Great Pyramid of Giza in Egypt, which is only 230 meters square at its base.

The Kofun Period produced two distinct types of pottery: Sue ware, based on Korean technology, and Haji ware, a native Japanese development. Korean potters migrating to Japan brought with them the revolutionary technology of the potter's wheel and high-temperature kilns, which made possible stronger, more durable and non-porous pottery called Sue ware. Sue ware was wood-fired and the extreme heat of the kiln melted the wood ash circulating within the kiln, some of which was deposited on the pots (**fig. 8, 83**). It is not known whether Kofun people liked, disliked, or were indifferent to these ash deposits.

From these Sue beginnings, the full decorative possibilities of natural wood ash deposits were not realized until 11–13 centuries later, in the pottery created at kiln sites, such as those in Bizen, Shigaraki, Iga and Tamba. Sue ware was made either by imported Korean potters or by Japanese potters instructed by Koreans. Production of Sue ware continued through the 11th century.

Haji clay was reddish yellow, low-fired, unglazed, porous, and largely used for the production of Haniwa, which included hollow clay figures. Haniwa were placed in rows on the outside of mound tombs. Their quantity varied from a few to over 1,000 on a single mound tomb (**figs. 6, 7, 33**).

From approximately the 6th century, virtually every aspect of Japanese life was subject to the overwhelming influence of China, including Buddhism, architecture, painting, sculpture, governmental organization, laws, calendar, written characters, Confucian thought, education, and even tax collection. This was not the forced result of military conquest. Japan sought to learn from the far more advanced Chinese civilization. Japan regularly sent large numbers of envoys and students to study Chinese institutions, culture and thought. When they returned to Japan, imitation to the point of copying commonly occurred. Significant innovation did not occur in Japanese pottery during this time. Through the 8th century, Sue ware remained the principal type of pottery produced. The more ambitious pottery still consisted of copying Chinese work, but the 9th century witnessed a slowing of Chinese influence and a concomitant rise in Japanese culture, identity and manners.

Chinese influence is not apparent in the 14th century pottery produced in the village of Shigaraki, located not far from Kyoto. It featured stunning, natural wood ash glaze storage jars (**fig. 82**). They were made by versatile farmer/potters during the time when their farm chores slowed, permitting pottery work. The taste for natural glazed pottery included pieces made in villages such as

6

FIG. 3. LATE JOMON PERIOD DOGU

FIG. 4.
MIDDLE JOMON
PERIOD DOGU

7

FIG. 5 YAYOI PERIOD

FIGS. 6, 7. KOFUN PERIOD

Bizen and Tamba. The growing popularity of Zen Buddhism, which emphasized rustic simplicity, lack of pretension and the Samurai spirit of frugality, furthered this new aesthetic.

Momoyama Period (1568–1603)

The Momoyama Period, comprising less than 50 years, from the late 16th century to the early 17th century, was brilliant, innovative, and of crucial importance to the history of Japanese arts, including ceramics. Its beginning saw incessant civil war and its terminus marked the approximate end of that chaos with the establishment of the Tokugawa Shogunate, which ruled for 265 years, until 1868.

In the blink of an historic eye, fundamental assumptions of ceramic art were questioned and overthrown. Luxurious, elegant Chinese ware was no longer the only gold standard. Instead, it was supplemented by two distinct aesthetic preferences, which have become recognized as quintessentially Japanese. The long-standing Japanese reverence for nature in all its infinite variety was transferred to the world of ceramics. Led by radical tea masters and Zen Buddhist precepts, the new aesthetic valued simplicity, the absence of fancy decorations, the natural wood ash deposits that fell during the kiln process, and even valued selective deformities of shape and cracks occurring in the hot kiln, which formerly would have meant discarding the piece. Respect for unpredictable nature was reflected in a new attitude toward accidents of ceramic making (**figs. 84, 85**).

Equally important, if not more important because of its far-reaching influence as the embodiment of artistic freedom, another development, Oribe ware, demonstrated a light-hearted irreverence toward tradition (**figs. 10, 111–113**). The long-buried taste for fun, fantasy, surprise and free spirits, was reflected in this new kind of ceramics which supplemented the older dominant taste for perfection in execution and form and overall seriousness.

Today, to fully appreciate the unique aspects of Momoyama ceramic art will require, for some, an adjustment of their aesthetic criteria. Perhaps it would be better or more accurate to say—a widening of their usual criteria. This should not be too difficult. It will not require swallowing some dubious abstruse academic theory of art, nor mastering torturous complex belief systems, myths, or the teeming iconography of Eastern religions. For some it may only require an open heart and a willing spirit.

A final word or two about the modern relevance of tea-derived aesthetics. Acts of appropriation and assembly, much in vogue in our contemporary art, were anticipated and practiced before and after the Momoyama Period. Antique Chinese ceramic vessels made for other purposes were removed by the Japanese from their original context and purpose and appropriated for tea use, transformed and assembled to function as tea utensils. Another basic Japanese aesthetic device, still in vogue, involves combining what are apparently quite different things which, nevertheless, work well together. This approach has broad application today, as evidenced, for example, by Japanese textile design, where seemingly odd combinations of patterns, colors and subject matter that Westerners would think insane to combine, are found not only to work well together, but to possess a fresh, dynamic, novel quality as a result of their unexpected successful imaginative juxtaposition.

Another important innovation during the Momoyama Period was Shino ware, probably developed by Japanese potters under the influence of white Chinese tea bowls. The resulting white Shino ware was, in the opinion of many, superior to the Chinese models (**figs. 9, 128, 174**). Most Shino pieces were made for the ritual meal before the tea ceremony, called Kaiseki, and for the tea ceremony itself.

It is easy to forget that 16th and 17th century painting in Western Europe was largely concerned with the most accurate copying of nature. Truth to nature was worshiped as an ultimate aesthetic value. Compared to Western art of the same period, Momoyama ceramic Shino and Oribe art, even though they drew from Japanese painting and textile design, were revolutionary breakthroughs. The faithful copying of nature was not a goal. Catching the essence of nature was a goal: distill the subject down to its beating heart; simplify by eliminating the superfluous; expressively highlight the significant; accept unorthodox compositions.

Edo Through Early Showa Periods (1603–1945)

Free trade advocates today might have a difficult time explaining the prosperity of the Edo Period (1603–1868). Edo is the old name for present-day Tokyo. In 1603, the Shogun, Tokugawa Ieyasu, the *de facto* ruler, established Edo, a small castle town, as the seat of his government, making it the *de facto* capital. The Emperor continued to reside in the legal capital, Kyoto. By the 18th century, with a population of over 1,000,000 people, Edo had grown to be one of the largest cities in the world, if not the largest. Yet Japan had a firm isolationist policy, banning until 1858 all foreign trade, except for minor Dutch and Chinese traders in the port of Nagasaki in Kyushu island. Foreigners were otherwise forbidden to enter Japan. All cultural contacts with the outside world were forbidden, including all foreign religions. Travel abroad by Japanese was forbidden. For approximately 100 years, all foreign books were forbidden.

However, domestic trade, agriculture and the merchant class all flourished. The arts of the theater and woodblock prints became elements of a growing, exuberantly optimistic popular culture. Ceramics followed this trend, turning away from sober, understated and unadorned work.

Depending on the definition of porcelain, it was either first produced in China in the second millenium BC, or was first made in 9th century Tang Dynasty China. Fortuitously,

in 1616, possibly an apocryphal date, a Korean potter who had been brought to Japan, discovered high-quality porcelain clay on the southern Japanese island of Kyushu. Perfectly timed, this discovery made it possible to ultimately produce in the late 17th century the highly decorative porcelain called Arita, which fit the new taste. Arita, the name of a Kyushu pottery-producing town, includes Nabeshima and Kakiemon ware, among other porcelain styles. Nabeshima is unusual in that originally it was not produced commercially, but was only made to be used by the local feudal ruler and his court, as well as for the ruler's presentation gifts (**fig. 14**). All Arita ware shared the qualities of being superbly crafted, having attractive subject matter and patterns, as well as gorgeous color. Kakiemon ware, a style of Arita ware that is still made today, eventually became world famous and was widely imitated (**fig. 13**). The Meissen porcelain factory in Germany was but one of many European manufacturers copying Kakiemon ware.

An enameled porcelain called Kutani ware was first produced in the mid-17th century (**fig. 12**). It was made in the Arita kilns on Kyushu Island, as well as in the western portion of Honshu, the main island of Japan. Still produced today, it is known for its distinctive colors, usually five: dark blue, purple, green, yellow and red.

The Tamba area just west of Kyoto produced storage jars (**fig. 11**). The use of Tamba ware in the tea ceremony never achieved the success of some other kiln areas.

During the 265 years of the Tokugawa Shogunate, Japan was effectively sealed off from the rest of the world. By eliminating potentially destabilizing foreign influences of every kind, and aided by a generally favorable domestic economy, the Tokugawa clan succeeded in maintaining its ruling power. However, after more than 200 years in power, the strength of the military Tokugawa Shogunate began to seriously erode. Rising debt and continuing internal struggles among local leaders weakened the Shogun. Then, in

FIG. 8. ASUKA PERIOD   **FIGS. 9, 10. MOMOYAMA PERIOD**

FIG. 11. EARLY EDO PERIOD

14

FIGS. 12, 13, 14. EDO PERIOD

1854, Japan was forced to accept trade with Western powers, another blow to the Shogun. This humiliating proof of the impotency of Japan's backward military and naval forces was the price it paid for its long isolation. It spurred greater, stronger opposition to the Shogun.

In 1868, Samurai from western Japan and certain court nobles succeeded in forcing the Tokugawa Shogun to cede power to the 16 year old emperor, who chose the name Meiji, or "Enlightened Rule." Although the Meiji emperor had little actual political power, he became the sacred embodiment of Japan as a unified nation. This era became known as the Meiji Restoration (1868–1912), signaling the fictitious restoration of power to the emperor. However, it is undeniable that the Meiji Restoration marked the end of feudal Japan and the start of modern Japanese history.

Meiji Japan, disdaining the usual intermediate stages, hurtled into the modern world of industry and technology with stunning success. The driving force was an extremely practical one: to create a modern army and navy equal to any Western nation in order to protect Japan from being dominated and controlled by the Western powers, as had already happened to the far larger China.

Within 45 years, Japan transformed itself from a pre-industrial agricultural nation to a modern industrial world power, both economically and militarily. In a total reversal, it not only tore down the walls excluding foreigners, it actively imported thousands of Western experts in engineering, military and naval affairs, education, government, business and industry, and sent commissions and students abroad to observe and learn. Japan also reached out to the West by exhibiting its arts and crafts, including ceramics, at international fairs, such as the Chicago World's Fair of 1893 (**figs. 15, 17**).

This highly-organized national effort produced newly-created modern capitalistic, industrial, commercial and trading firms, a universal educational system, a reformed tax structure, a modern railroad network and a powerful army and navy. So successful was this program that by 1895 Japan had, surprisingly, defeated China; Taiwan had become its colony; and in 1905 Japan defeated a Russian army and destroyed the Russian fleet. Japan also won control of Korea, which it annexed as a colony in 1910.

During its early stages, the breakneck speed of indiscriminate, fervent modernization threatened to sweep away centuries of tradition, including art works. Masterpieces of traditional Japanese art left the country with only a few local voices raised in protest. Fortunately the wave of uncritical enthusiasm for all things Western, and the failure of the Japanese to properly appreciate their own artistic heritage, was slowed by an unexpected force.

Ernest Fenollosa (1853–1908) was a 25-year-old Harvard graduate, brought to Japan in 1878 as professor of philosophy at the University of Tokyo. He became an enthusiastic expert on Japanese art. It was Fenollosa who worked to stop the massive outflow of significant ancient art works, chiefly paintings and Buddhist sculpture, and who tirelessly promoted the worth of Japanese art to the Japanese themselves, as well as to Americans. This did not prevent Fenollosa from amassing collections of Japanese art, which later became the foundation of the great collection at the Boston Museum of Fine Arts.

The runaway domination of industrialization was first challenged in late 19th-century England. Inspired by John Ruskin (1819–1900), art critic and reformer, and led by William Morris (1834–1896), a designer, the English Arts and Crafts Movement sparked a renaissance in crafts, home design, and textiles. The movement emphasized the importance of the craftsman in producing finer work in opposition to the lower quality products of industrialization.

In Japan, modernization also brought the introduction of mass-produced ceramics, calamitously reducing the demand for handmade pottery. Countless potters were thrown out of work, and artistic development, with some exceptions, was stalled.

In 1926, the Japanese Folk Art (Mingei) Movement was founded and led by Yanagi Soetsu (1889-1961), together with Hamada Shoji (1894-1978), (**figs. 162-165**); and Kawai Kanjiro (1890-1966), (**figs. 49-54**). It nostalgically looked back to a pre-industrial time, a time when regions were relatively isolated. It honored those anonymous potters who made practical ware for the everyday use of ordinary people. The ware was inexpensive. Its designs, regionally characteristic, were the result of the collective genius of generations of craftsmen. The Mingei movement succeeded in raising the appreciation of the beauty of folk pottery. It rejected the dominant Western ideal of the artist's individualism and independent spirit. Although it was influential, it fought a losing battle. Its ideal of collectivism could not stop the march of 20th century individualism.

The Meiji emperor died in 1912 and was succeeded by his son, Yoshihito Taisho (1912-1926). Yoshihito Taisho was very sickly and, after 14 years as the titular head of Japan, he was declared mentally incompetent and was succeeded in 1926 by his son, Hirohito.

Itaya Hazan (1872–1963)

The brief Taisho reign saw the rise of Itaya Hazan. He was a pioneer in the development of modern Japanese ceramics and in the triumph of artistic individuality. He was the first significant ceramist to receive art school training, a path that flourished and has continued to the present day. Also, instead of working in a collective kiln center, he was the first to become a studio potter in his own workshop. Hazan became recognized throughout Japan as a leading decorative ceramic artist. The course of his professional life became a model for future generations of potters (**figs. 18, 20**).

During the 1930s, Japanese potters, Arakawa Toyozo (1894-1985), (**figs. 129-131, 180**) and Kaneshige Toyo (1896-1967), (**figs. 86-88, 184**), found pottery fragments which led to their discovering Momoyama Mino and Bizen kilns. Other potters were inspired to make similar investigations of other ancient kiln sites, which also yielded fruitful results. Some potters were more affected by still earlier Chinese pottery, a foreign influence invariably filtered through a Japanese sensibility and somewhat transformed.

Tomimoto Kenkichi (1886–1963)

Tomimoto Kenkichi in 1955 was designated one of the first four Living National Treasures (**fig. 19**). He came from a wealthy family and spent two years studying in England before he returned to Japan to begin a successful and extremely influential career as a ceramist. Tomimoto founded the ceramics department at the Kyoto City University of Arts, where his teaching influenced generations of ceramic artists. He associated with Hamada Shoji, Kawai Kanjiro and Bernard Leach, and was a member of the Folk Art (Mingei) Movement. Tomimoto's insistence on the artist's individual creativity ultimately put him at odds with the Mingei ideal of the anonymous craftsman, and he withdrew from the movement.

Tomimoto also differed from the Mingei Movement by insisting that the potter's own hands should form the clay vessel; that the creative act required a totality of involvement in every phase, from beginning to end; that the artist/potter could not be a mere decorator of vessels made by an assistant. Tomimoto's career overlapped the radical changes in 1948 and thereafter in his own Kyoto backyard, when claywork was extended to include abstract sculpture. By stressing the crucial ingredient of artistic individuality, he helped prepare the way for the development of potters whose individual vision resulted in avant garde abstract ceramic sculpture.

FIGS. 15, 16, 17. MEIJI PERIOD

FIG. 18. ITAYA HAZAN, SHOWA PERIOD

FIG. 19. TOMIMOTO KENKICHI,
TAISHO PERIOD

FIG. 20.
ITAYA HAZAN,
SHOWA PERIOD

21

P. xi. Final Jomon Period

(1500–500 BC)

This figurine (Dogu) has survived in great shape. She sports a fashionable hairdo or hat; her large hips project fertility. This woman exudes the confidence in her strength that one would expect, considering her powerful legs and shoulders. Utterly defying anatomic reality, we see two small breasts arising from her shoulders and eyes that are below the level of her nose. Unfortunately, her elaborate tattooing or scarification remains mysterious, since we have no basis for arriving at an informed interpretation.

H. 7 in. x w. 4 3/4 in. (17.8 cm x 12cm). S.J. & G.W. Lurie Collection.

Fig. 1. Middle Jomon Period

(3500–2500 BC)

There is no mistaking its wild, festive spirit. Has any culture or society, before or since, ever made pottery of equal exuberance? If conveying ecstatic joy is a worthwhile achievement in art, this vessel is unsurpassed. Unfortunately, when looking backwards over several millennia, our ignorance and inevitable cultural distortions prevent any answer to questions regarding its purpose from being given with confidence. Were the Jomon expressing symbolic meanings where today we see only exuberant, overflowing forms?

H.14 3/4 in (37.5 cm). Nagaoka Municipal Science Museum.

Fig. 2. Middle Jomon Period

(3500–2500 BC)

Tightly organized and featuring neat concentric curved patterns in what is now called a lyre pattern, it exhibits rhythm coupled with classic restraint, suggesting graceful music. Perhaps Mozart.

H. 28 7/8 in. (73.4 cm). Yamanashi Prefectural Museum of Archaeology.

Fig. 3. Late Jomon Period Dogu

(2500–1500 BC)

We are drawn to her startled, perhaps fearful, eyes. Her unusual heart-shaped face is echoed in the negative space beneath her arms, each forming one-half of a heart. Parallel lines cover her arms, legs and part of her body, representing clothes or scarification. Is she wearing a ritual mask? We barely miss the absent hands, mouth and ears. Once seen, she is indelibly impressed on the memory.

H. 12 in. (30.5 cm). Tokyo National Museum.

Fig. 4. Middle Jomon Period Dogu

(3500–2500 BC)

This superb combination of human and cat families honors both. An unforgettable mysterious image, with stylized eyes and anatomically exaggerated sloping notched shoulders. The left arm and hand, or paw, is held to the breast in a quintessentially human gesture of sympathetic emotion, which is, however, mitigated by the commanding authority of the figure. The absence of the right arm makes it more difficult to interpret with any confidence the meaning of the left arm's gesture.

H. 10 in. (25.4 cm). Tokyo National Museum.

Fig. 5. Yayoi Period

(500 BC–250 AD)

Timeless in its appeal, it surprisingly achieves a beautiful silhouette by positioning a long, thick neck atop a thick body, tapering down to an unstable-looking narrow base. In the spirit of minimalism, two raised, encircling parallel lines are the only decorations on its body.

H. 13 3/4 in. (34.9 cm). S.J. & G.W. Lurie Collection.

Figs. 6, 7. Kofun Period

(250–552) Haniwa

It would be interesting to speculate why Haniwa figures always have appealing doll-like faces and hollow eyes, a temptation which we will resist. There is a hypnotic quality about the youthful innocence they project. They are endearing. The weapons they frequently wear do not inspire fear and appear more like part of a theatrical costume.

H. 52 1/2 in. (133.3 cm) and h. 44 1/2 in. (113 cm). Tokyo National Museum.

Fig. 8. Asuka Period

(552–710) Sue Ware

This vessel is notable for its thick but graceful curved long legs, which work well with the flattened belly and tall bell-like cover—all coated with splendid natural wood ash. Also see fig. 83.

H. 9 3/4 in. (24.8 cm). Kyushu Historical Museum.

Fig. 9. Momoyama Period

(1568–1603) Shino Ware

This water jar was made for use in the Tea Ceremony. It is decorated with freely-painted grasses, which give the piece a poetic quality. It embodies the liberated spirit of art in the Momoyama Period. Also see fig. 128.

H. 7 1/4 in. (18.4 cm). Hatakeyama Memorial Museum of Fine Arts.

Fig. 10. Momoyama Period

(1568–1603) Oribe Box

Today we see and accept this covered box with a multitude of images: two large wheels in water, weeping willow branches, an oversized grasshopper, flower petals, and, especially on the lid, lively patterns taken from textile design. But, when new 400 years ago, these decorations on pottery were without precedent. The effect must have been startling, even shocking. They probably appealed to the independent spirit of the new Tokugawa ruling dynasty, that was making a new beginning. Also see figs. 111–113.

H. 4 1/4 in. (10.9 cm). Private collection.

Fig. 11. Early Edo Period

(Early 17th century) Tamba Ware

Perfection of shape, color and size create an imposing presence, enhanced by an explosion of wood-ash, sprayed over a field of burnt reds.

H. 16 1/4 in. x diam. 11 1/2 in. (41.3 cm x 29.2 cm). S.J. & G.W. Lurie Collection.

Fig. 12. Edo Period

(17th or 18th Century) Kutani Ware

Characterized by signature colors, rigid geometric divisions, and tight rim organization, Kutani ware has proved to have a lasting, as well as an immediate appeal. The central spray of flowers set on blue and yellow rocks, enliven and soften the work. The central blue octagon reminds one of a Chinese scholar's window, through which are seen the outdoor flowers and rocks.

Diam. 14 1/2 in. (36.8 cm). MOA Museum of Art.

Fig. 13. Edo Period

(Late 17th Century) Kakiemon Ware

This attractive dish with auspicious subject matter looks back to Chinese models. The images include two Phoenix birds, a pine tree, plum tree and a bamboo tree—all symbolic of renewal, rebirth and new life. Also depicted are peonies, as symbols of prosperity.

H: 2.7 in. x diam. 13.8 in. (7 cm x 35.2 cm). Tokyo National Museum.

Fig. 14. Edo Period

(17th or 18th century) Nabeshima Ware

The decoration of this plate is largely derived from Japanese textile-based designs. The composition is notably dynamic and asymmetric, quirkily combining unusual subjects. This freedom of design probably reflects the unconventional taste of the ruling provincial lord.

H. 2 1/8 in. x w. 12 in. x d. 7 3/4 in. (5.4 cm x 30.4 cm x 19.8 cm). Suntory Museum of Art.

Fig. 15. Meiji Period

(1868–1912)

Vase With Flower And Bird Decoration, 1893. A charming vase by Taizan Yohei (1864–1922), featuring flowers arranged within a structure of wood. It was exhibited at the Chicago World's Fair of 1893.

H. 24 1/8 in. (61.3 cm). Tokyo National Museum.

Fig. 16. Meiji Period

(1868–1912)

A narrow-waisted vase by Ito Tozan (1846–1920), made early in the 20th century. Radically colored, the two blue bamboo stems are vividly positioned against an orange-yellow background. The bamboo echoes the curves of the vase, making a traditional theme compelling in a contemporary way.

H. 11 1/8 in. (28.3 cm). Tokyo National Museum.

Fig 17. Meiji Period

(1868–1912)

Vase With Hydrangea, 1893. A porcelain vase by Watano Kichiji (1860–1934), painted in strong Kutani colors. The head-on perspective view of the flowers and leaves hides the stems, giving a look of abundance and modernity. It was also exhibited at the Chicago World's Fair of 1893.

H. 24 1/8 in. (61.3 cm). Tokyo National Museum.

Fig. 18. Showa Period

Flower Vase With Design of Poplar Leaves. Late 1920s

Itaya Hazan's boldly decorated vase on a classical Chinese Meiping shape, with imposing broad shoulders and a somewhat stocky body. The brown leaf design was probably derived from Japanese textiles. Its leaf images are blurred by running brown glaze. Airless, these tightly packed images are individualized by yellow outlines and stems which run from the neck to the base.

H. 14.3 in. (36.3 cm). Idemitsu Museum.

Fig. 19. Showa Period

(1926–1989)

A 1960 Tomimoto Kenkichi jar is brightly decorated with four-petaled flowers in deep red, accented with gold. The excitement of this jar is generated by its repeated floral decoration, not its form.

H. 9 1/8 in. (23.2 cm). Museum of Modern Ceramic Art, Gifu.

Fig. 20. Taisho Period

(1921–1926) Itaya Hazan

A summit achievement in the decorative potter's art made in 1916. Departing from Chinese or Japanese predecessors, it reflects the vibrant genius of Hazan. The daring, vigorous, over-sized bamboo leaves are wrapped around the entire neck and body. The loosely-painted white and green leaves are stunningly set against a deep blue background, suggestive of a nighttime sky. But all is not perfect in this leafy paradise. Insects have devoured parts of some of the leaves, providing an obvious metaphor for human life as well.

H. 9 1/8 in. (23.2 cm). Idemitsu Museum of Arts.

Contemporary Ceramics: Post 1945
Introduction

Japan's rapid transformation to a modern industrial society has further accelerated over the last 60 years, creating contemporary Western-style cities, bursting with Western-style dressed inhabitants enjoying Japanese-enhanced Western-style techno-miracles. In some respects, Japan has already exceeded its Western models by creating, for example, inter-urban and intra-urban transportation systems that we in the West can only dream about.

After World War II, several factors arose which profoundly altered—and ultimately invigorated—ceramic making in Japan. Much of Japan was destroyed; its population was desperately poor, in a state of shock and, for the first time, forced to cope with the trauma of foreign military occupation. Long-standing political traditions were uprooted: the Emperor's position as a living god was seriously reduced, and a Western-style democracy and constitution were imposed. These rapid and bewildering changes caused profound national shock, then a spreading sense of uncertainty, which quickly engendered a generalized state of dissatisfaction. The old systems were seen to have failed and long-held values were challenged as obsolete.

Faced with this resulting void, many younger artists, galvanized by adversity, reacted positively, seemingly refreshed by these difficulties. They became energized with a sense that the times had created an unprecedented opportunity, actually demanded, that artists exercise their new freedom in their own field by shaking off the shackles of strict tradition. Tomimoto's teaching lauding artistic individuality was another factor enabling the tumultuous changes about to occur. Into this highly receptive atmosphere came further stimulation, as the work of great painters, such as Pablo Picasso (1881–1973), Paul Klee

(1879–1940), and Joan Miro (1893–1983), became known.

In 1947, an association of potters called Shikokai was formed in Kyoto. Its founder was the charismatic Uno Sango (1902–1988). Another founding member was the precocious Hayashi Yasuo (b. 1928). Many will be surprised to learn that in the late 1940s the schools of Japanese flower arrangement (Ikebana) were aggressively *avant-garde*. They actively encouraged and supported Shikokai members to explore challenging new forms, only incidentally, not primarily, designed to hold flowers. This helped give rise to truly sculptural expression in ceramics, in contrast to the vessel tradition. The most innovative result was quickly produced in 1948 by Shikokai's youngest member, Hayashi, then only 20 years old. His piece titled *Cloud* (**fig. 21**) is an overpoweringly muscular black glazed ceramic sculpture, whose parts swell almost to the point of bursting, with a small top opening. Nothing like it had been seen before in the entire history of Japanese ceramics.

In 1948, three other Kyoto potters formed another group called Sodeisha. Its articulate and aggressive leader was Yagi Kazuo (1918–1979), who had been making Korean-influenced pottery. The two other co-founders were Yamada Hikaru (1924–2001), whose work had been based on Song Dynasty Chinese ceramics, and Suzuki Osamu (1926–2001). Both Shikokai and Sodeisha members primarily wished to assert their freedom from past traditions in order to pursue fresh ideas. Sodeisha emphasized that they wished to avoid the judgment of others by refusing to participate in juried exhibitions, or exhibitions controlled by the government. They announced their inter-

FIG. 21. HAYASHI YASUO

FIG. 22. YAGI KAZUO

est in exploring the very nature of the entire ceramic-making process, its materials and forms. Some of their pottery, in other words, had as its subject matter the nature of pottery itself, much like the self-exploratory Western credo that art is, and should be, about art.

In actual practice, from 1948 until about 1954, Hayashi was the only member of either Sodeisha or Shikokai making abstract ceramic sculpture. Yagi and Suzuki were still making traditional Chinese-shaped flower vases, with large top-side openings, incised floral designs, or painted designs chiefly inspired by Klee, Picasso, Van Gogh, and Miro. It was not until 1954 that a Sodeisha member produced a work that properly could be considered an abstract ceramic sculpture rather than a vessel. In that year, Yagi made *Mr. Samsa's Walk* (**fig. 22**). This extraordinary object violated the function and appearance of vases; it had multiple openings, was unstable, had no definitive container volume, and its novel donut shape seemed propelled by weird short legs. The experience of it catapulted Sodeisha members into making ceramic sculpture.

In 1950, Kumakura Junkichi (1920–1985) produced some remarkable abstract ceramic sculptures (**figs. 39, 40**). At that time he was not a member of either Shikokai or Sodeisha.

To clarify the contributions of the leading artists, a special section, "Chronology of Abstract Ceramic Sculpture," charts the progression towards abstract ceramic sculpture by setting their work side-by-side for each year—1948 through 1954 (p. 29).

Another influence on the direction of ceramics came from an unlikely source. The post World War II economic boom in Japan set in motion a wave of new building construction. The law, highly conscious of preserving Japan's cultural heritage, required archaeological investigation, paid by the developers, when ancient artifacts were unearthed during the course of construction. This led to recovering large quantities of prehistoric pottery from Jomon and Yayoi periods, often of the highest artistic quality, which inspired a number of potters.

During this sensitive transitional period, Isamu Noguchi (1904–1988) came to Japan. He was the son of a Japanese poet and an American teacher. Noguchi was an older, artistically sophisticated key foreign artist who assimilated traditional Japanese clay techniques and forms. In 1950 Noguchi produced ceramic work in Seto, and in 1952 he worked with Kitaoji Rosanjin (1883–1959) and Kaneshige Toyo (1896–1967). Noguchi exerted considerable influence over young Japanese potters showing how contemporary international sculptural ideas could bc applied to ceramics.

In Japan, the age-old system for training potters, which involved long apprenticeships with a master potter, generally continued in the post-war period, but, importantly, was supplemented by university ceramic courses and ceramic training schools. Compared with potters who arose through the apprentice system, school-trained potters tended to favor the influence of international art movements, accelerating the rise of non-functional ceramic sculpture. This trend was reinforced by occasional exhibitions in Japan of contemporary Western ceramics.

Today non-functional ceramic art includes installation art, one of the current trends in international art. In recent years, some Japanese ceramists have been making installations. They are typically large-scale, room size. Some are entirely ceramic, others are mixed-media. Always composed of many different components, each may be important for understanding the whole installation. Still photography is woefully inadequate to provide meaningful images, and even less satisfactory as a vehicle for insightful comprehension. For these reasons, reluctantly, no installations have been included.

All this has led to the extraordinary position that ceramic art plays in contemporary Japan. Often referred to as a potter's paradise, Japan is the only country where the ceramic artist enjoys a high status and often a high income. The number of ceramic exhibitions held in each of the major cities of Japan is so large as to stagger the imagination of a Western art lover. Not only are there individual museums and art galleries devoted to ceramics, but many of the leading department stores throughout Japan have serious ceramic art departments with exhibitions that change weekly throughout most of the year. There are thousands of professional ceramic artists at work in Japan, artists who make their chief livelihood from the sale of their work. This unprecedented degree of acceptance and success depends on the large body of ceramic collectors who support this major artistic expression.

Although the field is still male-dominated, this situation is likely to change in the near future. Women today compose a majority of the students in some ceramic schools and are a significant minority in others. A few female ceramists already are professors in important schools, others are museum curators. In the highly gender-sensitive nation of Japan, this represents a, perhaps inevitable, Westernization.

It is sometimes said that Japanese ceramic history rep-resents 15,000 years of evolution, a word that implies improvement. We cannot endorse the view that there has been a clear aesthetic advancement since the unprecedented achievements of Middle Jomon and Momoyama Periods. Comparing eras is a very tricky business, freighted with assumptions and values both controversial and shifting. What weight should be given to originality as opposed to other qualities? How do you rate the degree of originality? Should applying international art ideas to pottery count as being original? These ungraspable difficulties lead to the conclusion that such comparisons are without much meaning or point. We prefer to say refinements over time, yes; changes, yes; expanded variety, yes; aesthetic superiority, invalid question.

The authors have been faced with the problem of how to organize the multitude of potters included in the Post-1945 Period. The artists we have selected show a mixture of local and international influences, various stylistic affinities, differing aesthetic purposes, making any systematic classification forced and false. Being unable to discover a truly satisfying formula, we have made the expedient choice to group some of the artists, somewhat loosely and somewhat inexactly, according to the geographic area of their kilns. The exceptions are those potters who are working in the distinctive Bizen, Shigaraki, Iga and Oribe styles, who we have grouped together regardless of where their kilns are located. This should facilitate a comparative study of certain styles.

Chronology of Abstract Ceramic Sculpture

We have not seen any evidence to cast doubt that Hayashi was the first Japanese abstract ceramic sculptor when he made *Cloud* in 1948 (see **fig. 21**)[2]. The accompanying chart (see p. 30) concisely illustrates the chronology.

What is less clear is the extent of Hayashi's influence on other ceramists, including Yagi, between 1948 and 1954, the date of Yagi's *Mr. Samsa's Walk* (see **fig. 22**). *Mr. Samsa's Walk* is the best known and the most influential work of post-1945 Japanese ceramic sculpture. However, an examination of the known physical circumstances and documented exhibitions in Kyoto, in nearby Osaka, and in other cities during the crucial six years between 1948 and 1954, suggest that Hayashi's importance may not have been adequately recognized.

According to Hayashi, during the period in question, Hayashi and Yagi both lived in the same pottery-making area of Kyoto called Gojozaka, approximately 150 meters apart; they both used communal kilns, sometimes even the same kiln, but different chambers, and they had mutual associates.

In 1948, Shikokai, Hayashi's ceramic group, organized four exhibitions, in which Hayashi showed his ceramic sculpture: in Kyoto, Okayama, and twice in Osaka, where *Cloud* was exhibited. In Kyoto, the exhibition was held at the centrally located art gallery of the national newspaper, Asahi Shinbun. The two Osaka exhibitions were held at centrally located art galleries in Hankyu Department Store and Daimaru Department Store. The Okayama exhibition was at a private gallery.

In 1949, Shikokai organized three exhibitions in which Hayashi's sculptural work was exhibited, including two in Kyoto and one in Okayama. The first Kyoto exhibition was again held at the Asahi Shinbun Gallery, and the second at the Gallery of Daimaru Department Store. A private gallery in Okayama was the site of the third exhibition.

In 1950, Shikokai arranged two exhibitions in which Hayashi showed his ceramic sculpture: in Osaka at the Gallery of Daimaru; and in Kyoto at the Marubutsu Department Store gallery. The Kyoto exhibition is particularly significant because it included a group of Isamu Noguchi's terracottas, along with four sculptural pieces by Hayashi. Noguchi was doing ceramic work in Japan in 1950 and 1952, and he and Yagi knew each other. Yagi later readily admitted that Noguchi's work greatly influenced him. Therefore, it seems likely that Yagi, as an ardent admirer of Noguchi and other Sodeisha group members, would have made it a point to visit Noguchi's show in Kyoto, at which time they undoubtedly saw Hayashi's four ceramic sculptures.

Also in 1950, the first post-1945 exhibition of Japanese contemporary ceramics in Europe was held at the prestigious Cernuschi Museum in Paris. It included a ceramic sculpture by Hayashi and a vase by Yagi, as well as work by Noguchi and other artists. The four-month Paris show was reviewed February 18, 1951 by the national Japanese newspaper, Mainichi Shinbun, which singled out

---

[2] Faulkner, Rupert. *Japanese Studio Crafts: Tradition and the Avant-Garde*. London: Laurence King Publishing, 1995. page 62; The National Museum of Modern Art, *Crafts in Kyoto [1945-2000]*. 2001, pages 8-49; Shigaraki Ceramic Cultural Park, *The Heart of the Creator in Contemporary Ceramic Art*. 1998. Pages 9-37; Todate Kazuko, *The Quintessence of Modern Japanese Ceramics*. Ibaraki Ceramic Art Museum. 2006. Page 10; Hayashi, Yasuo. *Chronology and related materials*, Kyoto: Hayashi Yasuo, 1987.

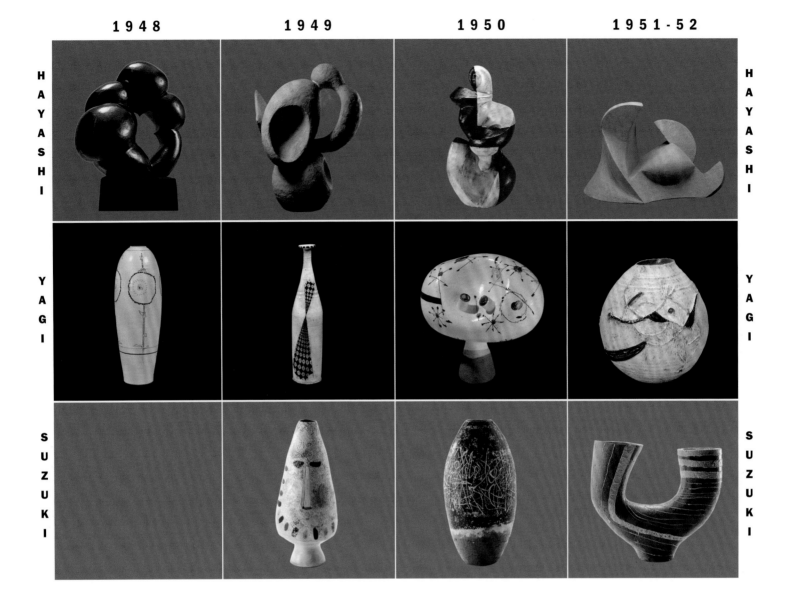

| 1948 | 1949 | 1950 | 1951-52 |

H A Y A S H I

Y A G I

S U Z U K I

only three artists for commentary about their *avant garde* pieces: Hayashi, Noguchi and Sango Uno, a founder of Hayashi's Shikokai group.

In 1951, Shikokai organized exhibitions in which Hayashi exhibited: in Osaka at the Art Gallery of Daimaru and in Fukuoka at the West Japan Newspaper Gallery. In 1952, Shikokai and Hayashi exhibited in Kyoto at the Art Gallery of Daimaru; in 1953, Hayashi exhibited twice in Kobe at the Gallery of Daimaru and at the Asahi Shinbun Gallery; and in early 1954, Hayashi exhibited in Osaka, as always, showing abstract ceramic sculpture.

The work Hayashi was showing prior to 1954 was often of remarkable quality: the 1948 *Cloud*, the 1950

and 1951 works illustrated in the accompanying chronology chart, and the *Sitting Figure* of 1952 (**fig. 23**). In the relatively small Kyoto world of Sodeisha and Shikokai members, their common associates and, perhaps, rivalry, Hayashi's advanced work, exhibited five times in Kyoto, five times in nearby Osaka, and twice with Noguchi's work in Kyoto and Paris—all before *Mr. Samsa's Walk*—could hardly have escaped notice by Yagi, other potters and curators. Finally, each of the exhibitions sponsored by Asahi Shinbun was publicized and announced in that newspaper. It may never be possible to know the specific impact Hayashi's imaginative work has had, but it may be a worthy subject for further scholarly investigation.

Pioneers of Abstract Ceramic Sculpture

Hayashi Yasuo
(b. 1928)

Hayashi is still extremely active as a ceramic sculptor. His creative energy continues even after his retirement in 1999 as an Art Professor at Osaka University of Art. Hayashi keeps his five electric kilns busy with multiple firings of his labor-intensive, hand-coiled works.

Fig. 21. *Cloud*, 1948. *Cloud* may be viewed (going counter-clockwise from the top of this photograph), as suggesting the head and the enormously muscled neck, right shoulder, arm and boxing glove of a massively strong and unbeatable champion. Of course, its title points to a completely different interpretation. A cloud, even a dark cloud heavy with potential rain and dust particles, is a wispy thing of fleeting duration that could not be more inappropriately depicted by the solid strength of this piece. The great exception could be that the black spherical masses relate to the Hiroshima atomic bomb death cloud, a mere three years earlier. Although Hayashi has expressly denied that he had that intention and association, we are free to choose our interpretation. Finally, the piece can be seen as a commentary on the balance between aggression and restraint. The six forms, although swollen with the inner power to burst outwards, are restrained by being bound together in a circular linkage. The tension from this ongoing struggle is obvious.

Its groundbreaking modernity is demonstrated by *Cloud's* possibly ironic title and its inhospitability to hosting a flower arrangement, or any other practical use of traditional vessels. Bereft of utility, severe, even brutal in form, it falls outside the conventional norms of pottery and decorative beauty. To those who were able to understand this achievement, *Cloud* could only be measured by the new standards its existence required and helped to create. It was, quite simply, an art object, an abstract ceramic sculpture whose significance and ambiguity was as difficult, contentious and provocative as the most interesting works of Western contemporary painters and sculptors using the traditional media of stone, metal and painted canvas.

H. 13 1/5 in. (33.5 cm). Misho-ryu Nakayama Bunpokai.

Fig. 23. *Sitting Figure*, 1954. This well-organized figural sculpture, born under cubist influence, has been stripped to the bone. Note the arched back, left shoulder and arm; buttocks and legs resting on a base. The head and legs are flexed toward each other, creating a tension like a spring near the point of release. At the same time we are drawn to the position of the head and face bending forward, an attitude of thoughtful concentration, an odd but intriguing coupling of ideas.

H. 23 1/5 in. (58.9 cm). Kyoto Municipal Museum of Art.

Fig. 24. *Gate*, 1978. We are given the privilege of looking through an arched temple gate into an inner sacred space. The spotted glazed exterior facade makes a clear separation from the interior space. It separates the secular world from the occult or spiritual world. A mysterious light glows on the floor of the passageway between the two worlds. The curious rear opening suggests a standing ghostly deity, or a guardian between the worlds. Whatever veiled meanings one may prefer, this work generates a fearful fascination. Hayashi has stated that the surrealism of Salvador Dali has been an influence. In this haunting piece, he has surpassed his influence.

H. 18 9/10 in. x w. 9 in x d. 11 1/2 in. (48 cm x 22.8 cm x 29.2 cm). S.J. & G.W. Lurie Collection.

Fig. 25. *Work 70-C*, 1970. This plain S-structure is a variation on a figurative theme. The head nestles on the shoulder. The rest of the body is modeled in compressed sculptural shorthand. On the evidence of the tubular construction, it bears an affinity to Fernand Leger (1881–1955). Has utter simplicity ever achieved more massive strength? Has strength ever been as successfully—with such minimal means—associated with tender softness? Can one conceive of any further reductions that would not destroy this image?

H. 16 7/10 in. x w. 13 in. x d. 10 1/2 in. (42.4 cm x 33 cm x 26.6 cm). S.J. & G.W. Lurie Collection.

Fig. 26. *Work 69-B*, 1969. Hayashi here invents another solution to the venerable art problem of how to harmonize curves and the rectilinear, not merely to co-exist, but to fruitfully enhance the work. This living sculpture is simultaneously reductive, yet evocative; rigid, yet flowing; abstract, yet representational. It suggests the somewhat tilted head of a woman with long, wavy hair.

H. 13 1/4 in. x w. 11 1/2 in. x d. 7 1/4 in. (33.6 cm x 29.2 cm x 18.4 cm). S.J. & G.W. Lurie Collection.

Fig. 27. *Focus 84-1*, 1984. A substantial body of Hayashi's work explores optical ambiguity. Hayashi had trained as a teenage pilot during World War II and was spared combat by the abrupt end of the war in 1945. He has stated that on nighttime training flights he sometimes became disoriented when he mistook a ground light for the taillight of another airplane, and was visually confused in trying to distinguish ground, horizon and sky. The memory of those experiences, together with the influence of cubism and surrealism, account for his preoccupation with intriguing visual and metaphysical uncertainties, in combination with basic geometric shapes. Hayashi explores the ambiguity between reality and illusion, interior and exterior, real and suggested depth, solid and hidden lines, the confluence of flat and curved surfaces, the contemplation and interactions of multi-layered, three-dimensional structural parts—in brief, with a host of intellectual and perceptual investigations involving the nature of reality. Unfortunately, the subtleties of Hayashi's optical works are particularly ill-served in photographs.

H. 12 1/4 in. x w. 15 3/4 in. (31.1 cm x 40 cm). S.J. & G.W. Lurie Collection.

Fig. 28. *The Sign of Memory*, 2001. Hello Miro and Surrealism! Apparently child-like in its innocent joy, the kite reaches the cloud at an ominous height. The kite is anchored to an elevated road or steps which lead to an unknown dark destination. Fear and pleasure are both generated.

H. 22 in. (55.9cm). Private collection.

Yagi Kazuo
(1918–1979)

Yagi was the eldest son of a ceramist, but, nevertheless, attended Kyoto Municipal School of Arts and Crafts graduating from its Sculpture Department. He also had a background in painting, metal work, glass, and a knowledge of international art movements. Yagi used his unusually broad training to become a versatile artist who produced important work in each of these fields, especially in ceramics.

Fig 22. *Mr. Samsa's Walk*, 1954. The character of Mr. Samsa appears in Franz Kafka's (1883–1924) story, "Metamorphosis". He awakes one morning to find that he has become a huge insect with many legs. Yagi's piece looks like a weird creature with stunted legs, without any recognizable human qualities, but not like the revolting insect of Kafka's story. In Yagi's piece, the stunted tubular legs refer in a more palatable form to Kafka's insect's legs. The circular shape of Yagi's work implies motion, a walk.

The great influence of *Mr. Samsa's Walk*, in part, came from its neat adaptability to important manifestos of rebellious ceramists. It could not be considered a vessel, although it had many openings, but none very practical. It was a parody of the traditional vessel that had a single opening. Although it made multiple references to the vessel form, in reality it discouraged its actual use as a container for flowers, or anything else. Yagi made the tubular legs on the potter's wheel, paradoxically using that traditional means for making a vessel, but simultaneously denying its necessity or practically. Yagi, hating the idea of being bound by conventional notions of beauty, deliberately used a wood ash glaze, that many would consider unattractive, to assert his independence from the past. Yagi's message was that the use of traditional material, clay, and a traditional technique did not doom the artist to making traditional pottery; he still had the freedom to make new forms, new sculpture. This opened a vista of creative opportunity which many followed.

H. 10 13/16 in. x 10 5/8 in. x 5 1/2 in. (27.5 cm x 27.0 cm x 14.0 cm). Private collection.

Fig. 29. *The Memory of Cloud*, 1957. Threatening spikes, top and bottom, are poised to envelop, sting and destroy. Aside from the subtle marks on its surface and the basic fact that it is made from clay, it makes no reference to traditional pottery—another declaration of Yagi's independence.

H. 20 in. (50 cm). Kyoto Municipal Museum of Art.

Fig 30. *Distant Entrance*, 1969. A visually striking, bronze-colored clay work, interesting enough for that reason alone. A staircase rises up from a barren surface to a window or door leading to the open air, an ambiguous destination. It suggests both the pointless vanity of ambition, fruitless hopes, a stairway leading nowhere, or, less convincingly to a Westerner, a stairway leading to open, infinite possibilities, the after-death paradise of conventional Japanese belief. The fact that the window or doorway is contained in a two-dimensional fragment, implying impermanence, that it is suspended in air and does not rest on anything solid—these factors tend to favor negative implications, possibly a lost post-war generation, or disillusionment with post-1945 art leading nowhere. Of course, rather than treating these alternatives seriously, it is also open to a humorous interpretation, in which the joke is that a stairway which is quintessentially functional, in this instance uselessly leads to no destination, except to an opening in a wall which, also quite ironically, supports nothing and separates nothing.

H. 13 1/4 in. (33.6 cm). Private collection.

Fig 31. *Black Echo*, 1978. Yagi shows us two highly abstract animate beings, which may suggest humans, with possible references to faces or heads. Is Yagi expressing a parable of the larger figure bending in humility, and the smaller figure prideful? The only things that seem to be clear are that the two are somehow relating to each other and that their sleek, shiny, elegant black forms engage our attention and pique our curiosity.

H. 15 1/2 in. (39.4 cm); h. 20 1/2 in. (52 cm). Hiroshima Prefectural Museum.

Fig. 32. *Work*, 1963. Severely pessimistic and brooding, it forces us to see wartime death and destruction, to see countless worm-like individuals crushed within a destroyed building. This tragic work may refer more broadly to the destruction of all hope, to the reign of disillusionment.

H. 18 1/2 in. (47 cm). The Museum of Modern Art, Kamakura & Hayama.

Suzuki Osamu
(1926–2001)

Another son of a potter who graduated from a ceramic school, Suzuki Osamu was influenced by a variety of international art movements, including cubism and abstraction, as well as by early Jomon figurines and Haniwas. He arrived at his own, highly-individualistic sculptural style in the 1960s with simplified, imposing forms of animals that projected warmth. In the 1970s, he began making celadon porcelain animals while also continuing his first signature style.

Fig. 33. *Haniwa Horse*, Kofun Period (250–552); **Fig. 34**. *Horse*, 1973. Suzuki's horse is turning its head, wondering how it became reduced to a massive cubist object, yet it seems content with its imposing presence. Suzuki's love of ancient Haniwas is apparent when we look at an ancestor of his horse in figure 33, a Haniwa horse.

H. 21 in (53.3 cm); h. 31 3/10 in (79.5 cm). Private collections.

Fig. 35. *Horse*, 1977. There is no denying that this is an extremely cute, but static, celadon pocelain horse, which reminds us of animals from toyland. The oversized body is decorated with fabric impressions. The undersized legs look like detachable toy legs. It shows us the technique by which it was made: two molded sections were joined together. The extra clay used to join the two halves is projecting above the head, neck, top and front of the horse. This explicit visual demonstration of the process of fabrication is a mannerism still currently much in vogue.

H. 19 9/10 in. (50.5 cm). Private collection.

Fig. 36. *Duet*, c. 1982. If we are guided by the title, then this is a rear view of two figures separated by a central line. At the upper left, there is a head with two eyes and a nose facing us; at the upper right, is a head in profile facing its neighbor. Picasso would understand these forms. The figures are wrapped in textiles which extend over two prominent buttocks and go down to the feet. There are elaborate decorations at the shoulder level. On the other hand, the title *Duet* may more accurately refer simply to two objects which have a passing resemblance to the human figure. This would overcome the strained interpretation of the heads, the absence of arms, and the missing two feet. Adding to the intriguing ambiguity, the surface is quite beautiful, with the shapes simultaneously cubistic and voluptuous, a difficult combination. Finally, there is about the entire piece a fond reference, both in color and in ash deposits, to traditional wood-fired Japanese ceramics, despite its being a sculptural, non-functional work of art.

H. 12 1/2 in. x w. 4 in. (31.7 cm x 10.1 cm). S.J. & G.W. Lurie Collection.

Fig. 37. *Bull*, 1975. A massive bull, built like a truck, ready to charge. Yet it stands on gentle, tiny legs, made of porcelain, is coated with a peaceful celadon glaze and armed with celadon horns! A playful contrast between the well-understood concept of a bull and Suzuki's parody.

Private collection.

Fig 38. *Clouds Above Mountains*, 1983. The title clearly tells us its subject matter. An overwhelming cloud hovers above the negative space in its center, which also can be seen as an abstract mountain. Wait a second! Could this be a ribald joke? Is this a rearview of an enormously heavy woman bending over, her two comically small breasts facing downward?

H. 17 3/8 in. (44 cm). Private collection.

Kumakura Junkichi
(1920–1985)

Although not widely recognized, as early as 1950, he was making abstract ceramic sculptures (figs. 39, 40). Kumakura avoided referring to traditional art works in any way. He was very much a man of his times, preferring to deal with contemporary social issues and contemporary concerns, such as sexuality and music, in a very aggressive, expressive, figurative style, which often was clearly erotic.

Fig. 39. *Work*, 1950. This is an example of Kumakura's early abstract ceramic sculptures. One thinks of the bare bones of an animal left to decompose in an open field; or a reclining figure beneath an oversized phallus; or simply a powerful formal composition.

H. 22 in. (55.8 cm). The Shigaraki Ceramic Cultural Park.

Fig. 40. *Work*, 1950. An abstract animal, highly cubistic in form, with enormous rear legs and buttocks, whose small head appears quite alert.

H. 12 3/4 in. x w. 26 in. x d. 10 1/2 in. (32.4 cm x 66 cm x 26.7 cm). Private collection.

Fig. 41. *Work,* 1970. It would be interesting to identify the musical score rakishly set on the dome, but, alas, we are unable to do so. The keyboard will bring the score to life. Most fascinating is the open mouth. Are we viewing the act of singing, or a sexual gesture? Music, after all, can simulate either or both. This unusual, high-impact work, shows us a face with only a single feature: a mouth with open lips. Not an individual portrait, it stands for every man and every woman. Since it is impossible to know whether we are seeing a singer or a person in ecstasy—it represents both.

H. 11 1/2 in. (29 cm). The Shigaraki Ceramic Cultural Park.

Fig. 42. *Castle of Jazz*, 1977. Attractive and repellent by turns, this sculpture is an unforgettable image and structure, dominated by disembodied, probably singing, thick lips. The eloquent top-most lips almost suffice as a substitute for the entire face. Its title includes the word jazz, indicating that we are seeing the lips of Black jazz musicians. The scattered severed fingers can be interpreted to reflect the birth of jazz out of the pain and suffering of Black people. The columns of the severed fingers and lips may refer to the generations, even centuries, of the cruelest hardships that Blacks have endured and which have triumphantly found expression in their music.

H. 25 in. (63.5 cm). Museum of Modern Ceramic Art, Gifu.

Fig. 43. *Figure*, 1977. Beneath the lacy gentility of her dress lies an uncontrollably voluptuous woman. Her dress does not hinder her availability, which has already resulted in pregnancy. Her hand gesture indicates a floating, calm contentment. The headless figure eliminates any likeness to a single woman and makes clear its application to all women.

H. 18 3/8 in. (46.6 cm). Museum of Modern Ceramic Art, Gifu.

FIG. 23. HAYASHI YASUO

FIG. 24. HAYASHI YASUO

FIG. 25. HAYASHI YASUO

FIG. 26. HAYASHI YASUO

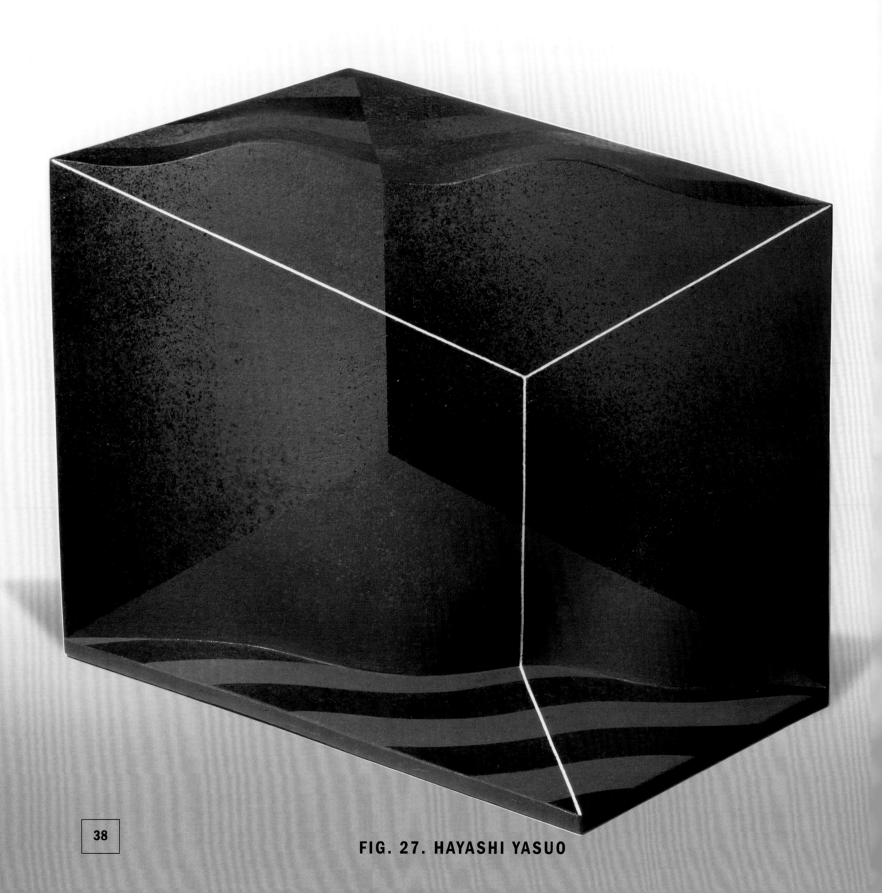

FIG. 27. HAYASHI YASUO

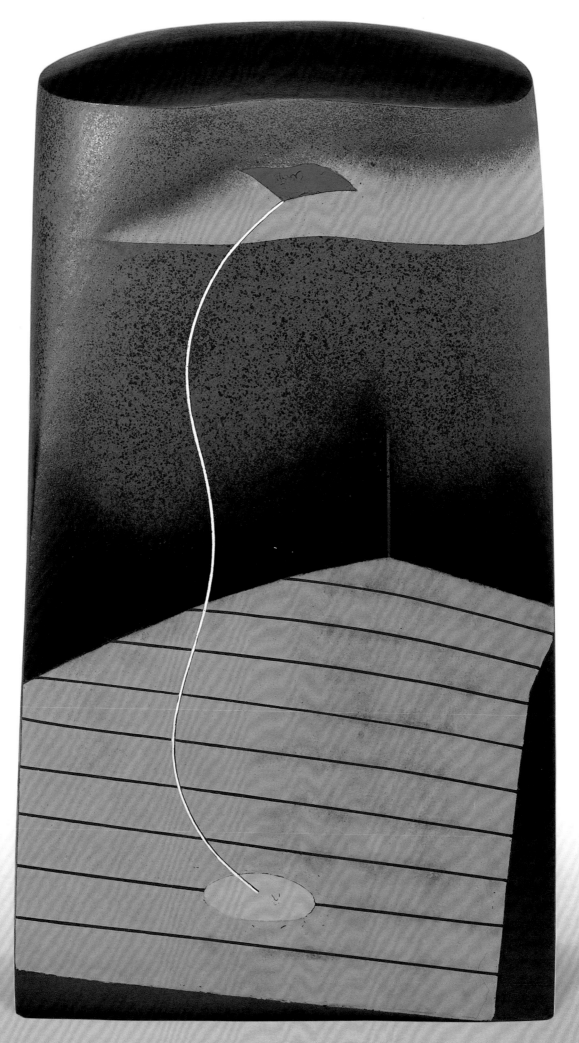

FIG. 28. HAYASHI YASUO

FIG. 29. YAGI KAZUO

FIG. 30. YAGI KAZUO

FIG. 31. YAGI KAZUO

FIG. 32. YAGI KAZUO

FIG. 33. HANIWA HORSE

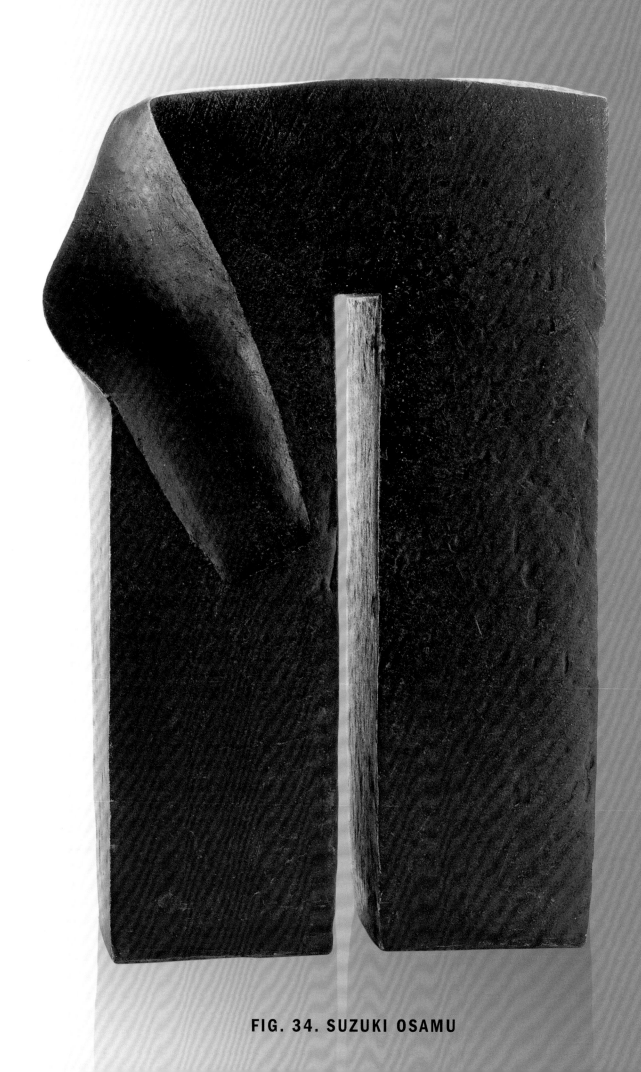

FIG. 34. SUZUKI OSAMU

FIG. 35. SUZUKI OSAMU

FIG. 36. SUZUKI OSAMU

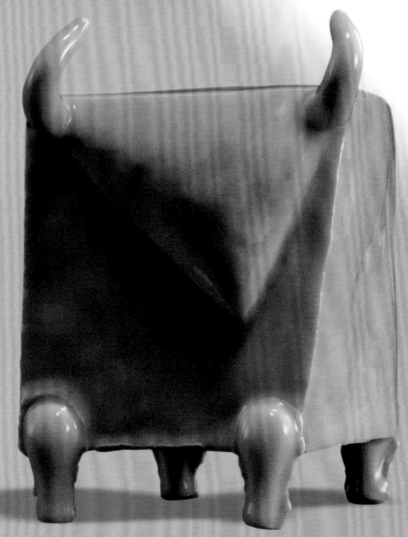

FIG. 37. SUZUKI OSAMU

FIG. 38. SUZUKI OSAMU

FIG. 39. KUMAKURA JUNKICHI
FIG. 40. KUMAKURA JUNKICHI

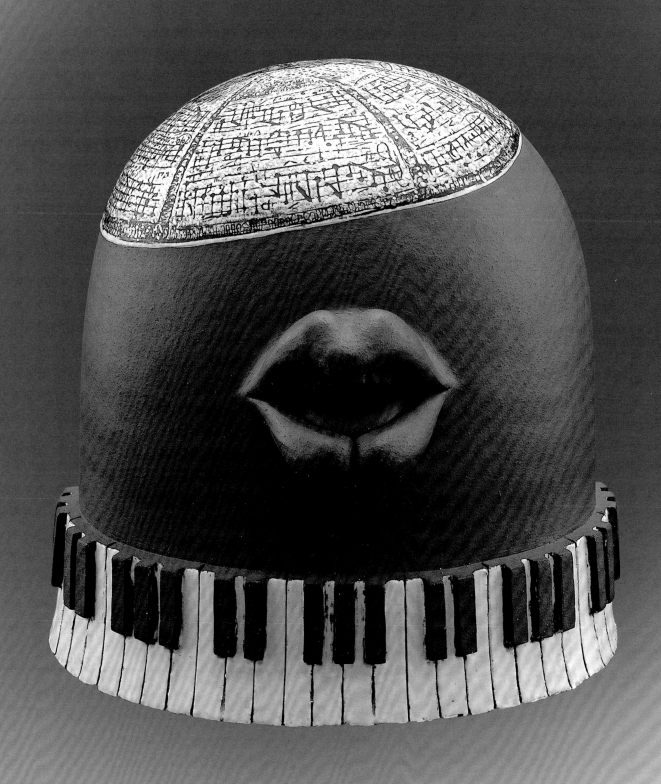

FIG. 41. KUMAKURA JUNKICHI

FIG. 42. KUMAKURA JUNKICHI

FIG. 43. KUMAKURA JUNKICHI

Kyoto Region

Out of respect for its irreplaceable historic architecture and art, Kyoto was not bombed during World War II. Close to 2,000 magnificent temples and gardens, plus some entire neighborhoods, still exist and transport one back to distant past times. These are not dusty dried out relics, falling to pieces, but rather are usually well-maintained functioning structures and areas that are actively and appropriately used. In brief, Kyoto remains one of the great destinations of the world for any sophisticated traveler.

Kyoto has been among the most important places for Japanese arts and crafts for about 400 years, being the favored working residence of many of the finest artists, ceramists, painters and other craftsmen. Kyoto has remained to this day a vibrant artistic ceramic center. Kyoto's rise to eminence is due principally to the work of two outstanding artists: Nonomura Ninsei (active 1646-1677) and Ogata Kenzan (1663-1743). Both avoided Chinese and Korean models in favor of applying Japanese painting techniques and subject matter to pottery.

FIG. 44. NONOMURA NINSEI

FIG. 45. NONOMURA NINSEI

FIG. 46. OGATA KENZAN

Nonomura Ninsei
(act. 1646–1677)

Nonomura Ninsei was born (date unknown) and raised in Tamba. He learned the potters' craft in Tamba, later moving to Kyoto. Ninsei's name is forever linked with the birth of Kyoto as a major ceramic center. Before Ninsei, overglazed enamel had been conventionally restricted to expensive porcelain clay found in the southern island of Kyushu. Ninsei innovated the use of overglazed enamel on high-fired stoneware which used an inexpensive clay readily available in Kyoto. Ninsei made it possible for Kyoto to develop its own profitable pottery industry using local clay.

Fig. 44. Edo Period (1603–1868). This incense burner is attributed to Nonomura Ninsei. The body represents a lotus seed, its lid a lotus leaf surmounted by a Buddhist lotus pod; Buddha's wheel is painted on the foot. Curiously, the lid contains Tibetan script. This beautiful burner is done with polychrome overglaze enamels with supplementary decorations painted in gold.

H. 10 1/2 in. (26.6 cm). The National Museum of Modern Art, Kyoto.

Fig. 45. Tea Jar with Design of Mt. Yoshino, Edo Period (1603–1868). Within a few decades after the close of the Momoyama Period, Ninsei painted high-fired stoneware inspired by earlier Japanese screen painting. On this tea jar he painted a utopian wonderland of colorful make-believe, softly curving mountains and wild flower scenery in a way that was undoubtedly popular and has so remained.

W. 5 3/4 in. x w. 6 1/16 in. (14.6 cm x. 15.4 cm). Fukuoka Art Museum.

FIG. 47. OGATA KENZAN

Ogata Kenzan
(1663–1743)

It is not clear whether Ogata Kenzan was inspired by his elder brother, Korin, a distinguished painter with whom he frequently collaborated, or Korin was more inspired by Kenzan. In any event, Kenzan brought an exceptional cultural background, which included poetry, painting and calligraphy, to his career as a ceramic artist. These other cultural interests delayed the start of his career as a potter until he was 37. He was famous and revered as an artist and ceramist in his own time, and his reputation has continued to the present day. Posthumously, in the 1960s, Kenzan became the focus of a stormy controversy as hundreds of pots, allegedly made by him, suddenly were discovered. Although it is not possible here, an extensive survey of Ogata's work can be extremely rewarding.

Fig. 46. Edo Period. (1603-1868) On this plate Ogata Kenzan has anticipated the work of a few of our contemporary artists, including Matisse's well-known paper cutout masterpiece, *The Snail*, now in London's Tate Modern Museum. Kenzan has created mosaic of jazzy forms that bounce, harmonize and interlock. He might well have been inspired by walls of stacked large stones that are commonly seen in Kyoto.

H. 14 in. (35.6 cm). Fukuoka Art Museum.

Fig. 47. Edo Period (late 17th c.-early 18th c.) A strong diagonal divides the striking decoration on this marvelous dish. The right side is decorated with an abstract summarily painted blue stream, flowing with impossible elegance. On the left, a bouquet of tightly arranged chrysanthemums amidst autumnal grasses beautifully contrasts with the openness of the blue water.

H. 1 3/4 in. x w. 11 3/4 in. (4.5 30 cm). Private collection.

Figs. 47A, 47B. This is another example of Ogata's continuing influence on contemporary art. At the upper left is Ogata's water jar with a handle. On the right side of the page is Rosanjin's Oribe vase with a handle (see p. 198 and **figs. 152-154** for Rosanjin). More than 200 years after Ogata's death, Rosanjin's piece seems not only to have been influenced by Ogata, but could have been an act of homage.

Ogata, Edo Period. H. 11.7 in. x 6.5 in. (29.8 cm x 16.6 cm) Itsuo Art Museum. Rosanjin, c. 1935-1954. H. 11.8 in. x 8.6 in. (30.3 cm x 22 cm) Private collection.

Ishiguro Munemaro
(1893-1958)

Ishiguro is notable for having lived a long, artistically productive and personally happy life. He was a devotee of Chinese calligraphy and Chinese poetry, and also found no problem in being a steady patron of Geisha houses, with a particular interest in Maiko, young Geisha trainees. Ishiguro worked with, and was influenced by, Kaneshige Toyo and Arakawa Toyozo. He exhibited widely in Japan, as well as in key U.S. cities. Famous for being well-dressed to the point of being a dandy, notably gregarious, his happy, active lifestyle is well reflected in the informal gaiety of this work.

Fig. 48. *Colored Jar*, 1959. Vivid impressionistic painting, makes this otherwise ordinary vase a work of decorative genius, impossible to forget. The abstract red persimmons, too vibrant, cannot be held in place by the organized network of black branches. The fruits break their black bonds and dance. The Japanese associate persimmon with autumnal nostalgia, knowing that the fruit will fade away at the end of its brief life cycle.

H. 7 3/8 in. (18.5 cm). Tokyo National Museum.

Kawai Kanjiro
(1890-1966)

Revered in Japan, but little-known in the West, Kawai Kanjiro was a friend and colleague of Hamada in founding the Japanese Folk Art Movement. Kawai's personal disdain of worldly honors and recognition, such as his refusal to accept the designation of Living National Treasure, reflected his ultimate wish to be left alone, free

to be an artist. He genuinely believed he was the mere instrument of a greater power which directed his work. The six works by Kawai illustrated are all from his mature years. By this time, Kawai, confidently working in a variety of styles, had traveled a great distance from his earlier interest in Chinese, Korean and folk pottery. His house in Kyoto is now a museum dedicated to his lifetime achievements.

Fig. 49. 1957. This plaque contains raised calligraphy in each corner: upper right: "hand"; lower right: "contemplating"; upper left: "foot"; lower left: "thinking." It is not clear what the large central raised image depicts. It may be a bird, the inner figure may be a flower with green and red petals. Other readings are possible and just how, if at all, they connect with the words in each corner, is another mystery. Considering Kawai's dedication to his art, we prefer the following interpretation. The foot propels the potter's wheel; the hand shapes the clay; contemplating and thinking are key ingredients of the creative process. In any event, the plaque is attractive, enigmatic and provocative.

H. 13 in. (33 cm). The National Museum of Modern Art, Kyoto.

Fig. 50. *Vase*, 1964. Using his signature cobalt blue glaze, Kawai surprises us with unusual triple spouts on this molded vase. The spouts provide a lift to the heavy body, and vie with the body motif for our attention. The large spouts may be the remote descendants, much transformed, of the elaborate Middle Jomon vessel rims.

H. 9 1/4 in. x w. 8 1/2 in. (23.5 cm x 21.6 cm). S.J. & G.W. Lurie Collection.

Fig. 51. *Ash Glazed Vase With a Raised Bird Design*, 1953. Kawai decorated this uniquely shaped molded vase by outlining bird shapes with a raised, white glaze. He filled in the bird forms in radical black, green and red colors. They are arranged imaginatively, rejecting the canons of strict realism, and are especially dynamic, multi-directional.

H. 16 in. x diam. 12 in. (41.0 cm x 31 cm). Private collection.

Fig. 52. 1955. Stormy, swirling, ferocious water covered with cobalt-blue glaze, it becomes a vortex of dramatic white crests. Kawai's own hand, sweeping across the surface, has imparted a visible personal energetic dash.

Diam. 12 3/4 in. (32.4 cm). Kawai Kanjiro's House.

Fig. 53. *Flower and Hand*, c. 1960. The hand is holding a lotus flower, with three fingers pointing skyward. The lotus plant is rooted in muddy waters, a metaphor for our very imperfect world. It grows out of its muddy beginnings up into the free air as a beautiful, purified flower, symbolic of enlightenment, moral clarity and overcoming base origins. This image reflects Kawai's ultimate artistic goal.

H. 17 1/10 in. (43.4 cm). The National Museum of Modern Art, Kyoto.

Fig 54. *Three-Colored Bottle*, 1962. Made by pouring or throwing three different colored glazes onto a molded bottle, it is reminiscent of American abstract expressionist art, particularly the action painting of Jackson Pollock (1912–1956). It conveys energy. In his last years, Kawai painted with a youthful freedom, as he did in this piece.

H. 8 $\frac{1}{2}$ in. x w. 12 $\frac{1}{4}$ in. x d. 7 $\frac{1}{4}$ in. (21.6 x 31.1 cm x 18.4 cm). Kawai Kanjiro's House.

Tsuboi Asuka

(b. 1932)

Tsuboi is, undoubtedly, the leading feminist ceramic artist in Japan. She arrived at this role through an unusual path. Born in Osaka, she trained under Tomimoto Kenkichi as a potter in tradition-bound Kyoto, in spite of its anti-female environment. Women were considered unclean and physically too weak to become potters. Adding to those obstacles was the special prejudice against one born outside of Kyoto and not accepted as part of the tightly closed Kyoto circle. In protest, she founded the Women's Ceramic Association in the late 1950s.

Reinforcement of her feminist convictions came in 1966 when she visited China for fifty days during the Cultural Revolution. She witnessed the atrocious destruction of much of China's cultural heritage, and the diabolical use of self-criticism to humiliate and brainwash the intelligentsia. Tsuboi managed, however, to extract a positive beneficial use from the technique of self-criticism by deepening the questioning of her own fundamental goals as a potter. She returned to Kyoto even more determined to address contemporary feminist concerns. True to her convictions, almost everything she has created since that time has as its subject some aspect of a woman's life expressed metaphorically.

Fig. 55. *Fruits of Pleasure*, 1972. One's eye is immediately attracted to the apple and the stacked breasts, an obvious reference to Adam and Eve. The breasts emphasize the prodigality and power of the enticing female body. The erect red nipples imply sexual pleasure. Completing Tsuboi's celebration of female sexuality, arguably, the breasts form a vaginal opening.

H. 25 $\frac{1}{2}$ in. (65 cm). The National Museum of Modern Art, Kyoto.

Fig. 56. *Summer Festival*, 2006. Too often women, confined by society to domestic activities, have not been credited with possessing high artistic sensibility because they were discouraged from exercising that ability as painters and sculptors. Tsuboi seems to argue that a woman's choice of a fashion accessory, a handbag, is not necessarily a trivial decision involving a trivial object. She demonstrates that a handbag can be regarded as a piece of wearable sculpture and that her selection is an exercise of her aesthetic judgment. The true worth of the handbag is suggested by its being colored in precious gold and silver. By adding a real fabric tassel to the ceramic handbag, was Tsuboi acting like those art theorists who proclaim they are blurring the distinction between art and life?

H. 12 in. x diam. 11 $\frac{1}{2}$ in. (30.5 cm x 29.2 cm). S.J. & G.W. Lurie Collection.

Fig. 57. *Brocaded Memory—Thinking of Tofuku-ji Temple*, 2005. Tofuku-ji Temple, next to the artist's home, is one of the most beautiful Zen Buddhist temples in Kyoto. It is especially famous for its autumnal leaf viewing. Thinking about the beauty of Tofuku-ji Temple may lead to contemplating other forms of beauty, notably the beauty of women and the beauty of the textiles that adorn women. No one would make the mistake of regarding this as a vase, although the top is wide open. Rather, we sense the presence of a woman, despite the fact that no bodily part is depicted. She is richly dressed, wrapped in a magnificent silky textile, and one can almost hear the rustle of her dress. Kyoto's glorious textiles are here expressed in clay. The piece is tied in two places, a possible comment on the constrictive and subservient role of women in society. Nevertheless, we know for a certainty that this is an absolutely beautiful woman, full of well earned pride and dignity. Lastly, we cannot overlook that Tsuboi has made a resplendent sculpture with dramatic drapery-like folds, whose shapes and shadows activate the surface.

H. 23 $\frac{1}{2}$ in. x diam. 12 $\frac{1}{2}$ in. (59.7 cm x 31.7 cm). S.J. & G.W. Lurie Collection.

Fig. 58. *Kyoto Dance*, 1988. This is another aspect of Tsuboi's interest in handbag imagery and Kyoto textiles. This type of handbag is in common use and consists of a bamboo or wood body with an attached fabric top. Tsuboi expresses both the rigidity of the body and the fluidity of the fabric top. She proceeds to engage in imaginative improvisation on the handbag theme. The fabric top, like the outfit worn by a dancer, is made from Kyoto's textiles. The "T" shape of the handbag echoes the shape of a kimono. Here the "kimono sleeves" flair out in time with the music to give the impression of a woman dancing—as the title of the work makes explicit. Dynamically colored diagonals reflect the soaring notes of the music and the graceful, sweeping motions of the dancer. A lady's handbag has been confirmed as a legitimate vehicle for artistic expression.

H. 10 in. x w. 9 in. x d. 7 $\frac{1}{5}$ in. (25.4 cm x 22.9 cm x 18.3 cm). S.J. & G.W. Lurie Collection.

Fig. 59. *Girl Sending Message*, 2003. A thick zig-zag bolt enters through the center of a pile of six breasts. Is this a lightning bolt, a phallic symbol, a combination of both depicting the power and pleasure of the sexual act, or is the "message" the girl is sending about her new-found freedom to be more active, and have careers? The artist has said that her intention is to depict the social changes that have occurred in women's lives. In her youth, women were quiet, conservative and moderate. Now, as implied by the dynamic zig-zag bolts, they are more active, drink, often speak loudly, have fun and party. The breasts, nipples erect, seem to excitedly accept the bolt. The precious quality of women's breasts is recognized by their gold and silver color. The message the girl is sending is the pleasure of sex for both male and female. This is a recurring theme of Tsuboi, whose candid imagery repeatedly endorses female freedom.

H. 28 1/2 in. x 25 1/4 in. x 25 1/4 in. (71 cm x 63 cm x 63 cm). Private collection.

Fukami Sueharu
(b. 1947)

Fukami has enjoyed a meteoric rise, gaining both critical and popular success. His reputation in Japan and the West may exceed that of any other living Japanese ceramic artist. He has admittedly been inspired by Chinese Song Dynasty (960–1279) porcelain, to the point where he now works exclusively in the celadon porcelain medium. Fukami's technique consists of injecting liquid clay under high pressure into plaster molds, making limited editions of usually no more than eight. He also produces one-of-a-kind pieces. Fukami takes particular pride in his impeccable, flawless surfaces. He has rejected, as being nothing more than an elaboration of the obvious, the fashion of leaving hand or finger marks on surfaces, which he considered a cliche, currently rationalized as demonstrating the handmade process. Fukami strives to achieve his ideal of pure, elegant forms and surfaces, an intense pursuit of perfection to convey transcendence, exaltation, nobility.

Fig. 60. *To the Sky*, 2002. A moment in the flight of a moving abstraction or a rolling sea, whipped by the wind towards the sky, breaking the sublime stillness.

L. 35 in. x d. 9 1/8 in. (88.9 cm x 23.1cm). S.J. & G.W. Lurie Collection.

Fig. 60A. A detail of Fig. 60.

Fig. 61. *Scene*, 2003. This epitomizes Fukami's ultimate goal of celebrating a virginal purity, the freshness of pale blue celadon, and absolute elemental forms, that are, nevertheless, emotionally expressive and symbolic. *Scene* cannot fail to inspire a kind of idealism, co-existing uneasily with its resemblance to the blade of a sword. This provocative combination, unfortunately, reflects the realities of our time, or all times, in which ideals are made to serve violence and war.

H. 49 7/8 in. x w. 8 1/2 in. (126.7 cm x 21.6 cm). S.J. & G.W. Lurie Collection.

Fig. 62. *Sky in the Morning*, 2003. Fukami's childhood memory of the beautiful curves of temple roofs inspired him when he created this one-of-a kind box. The three-lay-

ered pagoda roofs are compressed, forming a lyrical uplifting lid in tension with the mass of the diamond shaped body. The roofs and body of this celadon temple offer the promise of heavenly comfort and peace.

H. 7 1/2 in. x d. 7 5/8 in. x l. 11 3/4 in. (19.1 cm x 19.3 cm x 29.8 cm). S.J. & G.W. Lurie Collection.

Takiguchi Kazuo
(b. 1953)

Takiguchi Kazuo has created living, breathing organic sculptural forms. At his best, his forms have an incomparable subtlety and originality, and cannot be confused as the work of any other ceramist, past or present. While sculptural in intent, his forms nevertheless have vestigial or even large openings which provide evidence that he is still mindful of the traditional vessel form. Each piece gives a sense of swelling from internal activity, as if inhabited by a life within. Takiguchi said it best: "My works seem to move around as if they were little creatures who used to live there . . . they have started a new life, away from my hands." When his pieces are seen in the round, they reveal continuously changing, energized forms. They gain when seen together in a group, seeming to be in communication. The sometimes subtle and sometimes obvious voluptuous forms may invite tactile exploration. One would be challenged to withhold admiration for his rich and varied surfaces.

Fig. 63. *Untitled*, 2001. Two rising animate forms butt against each other at the top. Both have powerful shoulders bulging with effort and metallic-like skin. Their struggle is at a stalemate, while they catch their breath. It will recommence any moment. Although resembling no known creature, there is no difficulty in believing that each form is somehow alive.

H. 16 1/2 in. x w. 21 1/4 in. (41.9 cm x 53.9 cm). S.J. & G.W,. Lurie Collection.

Fig. 64. *Untitled*, 1999. Unusually explicit for Takiguchi, this creature is a strange living thing, an oddly voluptuous animal, with breasts, three legs and deep-grey skin. Whatever it may be, its erotic quality is uncomfortable, eerie and unsettling, as illustrated in the detail.

H. 10 in. x l. 17 in. x w. 14 1/2 in. (25.4 cm x 43.2 cm x 36.8 cm). S.J. & G.W. Lurie Collection.

Fig. 65. *Untitled*, 2001. Takiguchi here overcomes the difficulties of inventing a convincing, original organic form. The massive, fearsome tripartite creature lumbers forward while making surprisingly delicate contact with the ground.

H. 14 in. x w. 21 in. x d. 11 1/4 in. (35.6 cm x 53.3 cm x 28.6 cm). S.J. & G.W. Lurie Collection.

Fig. 66. *Untitled*, 2000. This object captures a dramatic and beautiful moment in which the boldly extended front leg is theatrically pulling away from the two short rear legs, as in the fluid movement of a dancer.

H. 7 5/8 in. x l. 16 1/8 in. (19.3 cm x 40.9 cm). S.J. & G.W. Lurie Collection.

Hinoda Takashi
(b. 1968)

Hinoda is among the youngest generation of professional ceramic artists. He is obviously influenced by comic books, cartoons, animated films and a pop art. Within these influences, his work demonstrates a stylistic versatility: cartoon imagery (fig. 67); a humanoid creature (fig.68). Hinoda has consciously avoided what he regards as the gloominess of too many traditional Japanese potters. Without changing his bright colors and funky forms, Hinoda has already given evidence that deeper qualities are to be found in his work. His light touch is not inconsistent with an underlying seriousness of purpose.

Fig. 67. *Untitled*, 2002. Hinoda has said that he intentionally avoids a single thread of meaning, that his pieces are not as simple as they look and that he often consciously wishes to make viewers feel uncomfortable in order to provide stimulation. Those purposes are all realized in this work. Two stylized heads—probably, but not certainly—human, have intertwining tubular bodies. Are they relaxing, mating or fighting? The single feature on the heads, a huge indentation, expresses exactly what: whining, screaming or something else? The rough texture encourages "feeling with your eyes," as Hinoda has remarked. We experience a growing uneasiness as we try to understand whether this cartooney figure is funny and cuddly or menacing.
H. 20 1/2 in. (52.1 cm). S.J. & G.W. Lurie Collection.

Fig. 68. *Rush Hour Zombie*, 2004. Thirty teeming, stressed-out men and women pour out of a bleak, grey-black subway station or building. They range in expressions from unhappy to terrified. They appear to be going to, or coming from, a dreadful place. These are mostly men dressed for business. This work constitutes a biting commentary on the unhappy life of even prosperous corporate employees. Hinoda's social commentary is done in a palette of very personal colors, an exaggerated perspective and expressive distortions of size.
H. 13 in. x w. 19 in. x d. 14 3/4 in. (33 cm x 48.3 cm x 37.5 cm). S.J. & G.W. Lurie Collection.

Yamazaki Akira
(b. 1927)

Born in Kyoto, where he still resides and works, Yamazaki has exhibited internationally and has been an exceptional prize winner in ceramic competitions in Japan. He is particularly interested in expressing what can be regarded as the quintessential Japanese sense of beauty, paying particular attention to subtleties of color, form and texture. Yamazaki is a quiet, modest artist whose personality is reflected in the delicate beauty of his work.

Fig. 69. c. 1983. Like an early morning mist, the diffuse green glaze rises over a pale yellow background. This full-bodied vessel appears tender and soft. The two tiny spherical ears somehow manage to balance the body.
H. 8 1/2 in. x diam. 10 3/4 in. (21.6 x 27.3 cm). S.J. & G.W. Lurie Collection.

Fig. 70. 1981. This large plate tells the life story of a young leaf. At its birth, it is a finely crackled tender yellow; as it develops, it shades into a youthful green, finally maturing into a deep green. What cannot be conveyed in a photograph is its delicious surface, which almost invites caressing. A detail is shown alongside the plate.
Diam. 19 1/2 in. (49.5 cm). S.J. & G.W. Lurie Collection.

Miyashita Zenji
(b. 1939)

Mountainous landscapes receding into a distant sunrise are continuing themes of Miyashita Zenji's work. Or, more broadly interpreted, his subject is the effect of light—or enlightenment— on sharply delineated forms receding into the far distance. Miyashita painstakingly applies thin layers of overlapping colored clay onto a clay body, achieving gradations of color, which create corresponding raised layers.

Fig. 71. *From the Sea to the Sky*, 1990. Deep blue mountains in the foreground gradually modulate to more distant mountains in lighter colors as they rise to the top of the work, climaxing in bright yellow and red sunshine.
H. 16 1/2 in. (41.9 cm). Private collection.

Fig. 72. *Vase*, 1990. Miyashita uses the same technique on a phallic-shaped vessel, or is it a headless torso, or is it best understood as simply an interesting form? Streams of color flowing downward shade from lighter to darker.
H. 19 1/2 in. (49.5 cm). S.J. & G.W. Lurie Collection.

Morino Hiroaki Taimei
(b. 1934)

Morino's talents were recognized early, and while still a young man he was invited to teach ceramics at universities in the U.S.A. His works are always decorated in a way that shows a consistent taste for emphatic formal clarity, with abstract, not representational patterns. In Morino's hands, his simple geometric shapes fit comfortably with the poetic aura his work may evoke.

Fig. 73. *Lagoon, Silver Glazed Pilgrim Flask*, 1989. Imagine clear, silvery water outlined in fresh green, flowing through darker gray and still darker gray backgrounds, along with stylized musical notation. Only a few, but important, dancing notes are indicated—just enough to allow us to hear the bucolic music.
H. 14 3/4 in. x w. 13 in. x d. 8 in. (37.5 x 33 x 20.3 cm). S.J. & G.W. Lurie Collection.

Fig. 74. *Black Glazed Vase with Ear*, 1982. Morino here shows an interesting combination of influences. His decision to place a handle on only one side of the triangular-shaped vessel reflects the Japanese aesthetic of asymmetry. The black and orange color combination is reminiscent of pre-

Hispanic Southwest American Indian ceramics. The black forms vaguely suggest primitive symbols.

H. 9 3/4 in. x diam. 8 1/8 in. (24.8 cm x 20.6 cm). S.J. & G.W. Lurie Collection.

Fig. 75. *Blue Sea Vase with Hock Shaped Design*, 1989. Dreamy, slowly falling light blue droplets against a dark blue central passage that meanders between golden verticals with eccentric branches. Mysterious and darkly poetic in Morino's unique style.

H. 11 in. (27.9 cm). Private collection.

Miyanaga Tozan III (Rikichi)
(b. 1935)

Miyanaga comes from a 100-year-old potters' family and lives and works in Kyoto. He studied in the sculptural department of the Kyoto City Art University, after which he came to New York and studied at the Art Students League. Aided by his sophisticated background, Miyanaga is a ceramic virtuoso finding new ways of expressing the age-old beauty of cobalt-blue glazed porcelain. In traditional blue and white porcelain, blue was used to draw designs on a white ground. Instead, Miyanaga uses shades of a special blue as the sole surface color.

Fig. 76. *On the Way*; **Fig. 78.** *Mountain in the Moon* (both made after 1990). The special blue surfaces of all three sculptures create a mood best described as other-worldly, and are surprisingly lyrical. **Fig. 77.** *Vallcy*, made after 1990, a triangular form, may be better seen as a spiritual blue mountain for the exclusive use of dedicated visionaries seeking revelation of higher truths. Miyanaga enjoys creating optical ambiguity by simultaneously crafting the real depth of through-and-through holes, lesser but real carved-out shallow depths, and, most interestingly, other areas that only give the illusion of depth. This illusion is accomplished by blowing differing layers of blue glaze onto an even surface. The overall effect is of solid, clear abstract forms, colored in an intriguing, intense blue, that can be extremely evocative.

Fig. 76. H. 20 in. x w. 17.3 in. x 7.4 in. (51 cm x 41 cm x 19 cm). Private Collection.

Fig. 77. H. 16 in. x w. 17 in. (40 cm x 43 cm). Private Collection.

Fig. 78. H. 19 in. x w. 16 in. x d. 17 in. (48 cm x 40 cm x 17.5 cm). Private Collection.

Shigematsu Ayumi
(b. 1958)

Shigematsu Ayumi, born in Osaka and now living and working in her studio in nearby Kobe, is a graduate of Kyoto City University of Arts, where she studied with Suzuki Osamu. The direction of her work, however, has differed sharply from his. In 2002, she became the first female ceramic professor at her *alma mater*. She is among the vanguard of women who have become influential in molding a new generation of ceramists, who, in increasing numbers, are women. It is surely the strength of her work, and not mere political correctness, that has enabled her to reach her position of academic importance.

Fig. 79. *Ferengi*, 2000; **Fig. 80.** *Parasite*, 1998; **Fig. 81.** *Ear's Bone*, 1996. At the present time she begins by making small models. Her work takes on an organic appearance, often arising from a small base and growing, growing upwards. She has characterized her creative process as "thinking with one's hands," rather than making aesthetic choices exclusively with her mind. Her forms suggest female body parts, internal organs and vegetation. Some of the pieces illustrated are highly sexual, with multiple swelling breast-like shapes and, in one piece, showing an aperture which bears resemblance to both an ear and to female genitalia. Her colors are not realistic. Shigematsu prefers an array of pastel colors, highly unusual for ceramics. This represents a significant rebellion against the norm that clay work should only look like clay. Further, their un-clay appearance is enhanced by their super-smooth surfaces, burnished or shining in a way that may look more like plastic than clay. She is another contemporary artist making clay sculpture that defeats one's expectations of what clay works should look like. The impact of her forms and colors suggest voluptuous, attractively-colored forms. Complex associations and aesthetic daring mark Shigematsu as a challenging artist.

Fig. 79. H. 67 in. x w. 11 in. x d. 7 in. (171 cm x 27 cm x 17.5 cm). Ibaraki Ceramics Museum

Fig. 80. H. 28 in. x w. 10 in. x d. 11 in. (70.5 cm x 26 cm x 27 cm). Tokyo National Museum of Modern Art Collection.

Fig. 81. H. 9.1 in. x w. 24 in. x d. 18.3 in. (23.2 cm x 61 cm x 46.5 cm). Shigaraki Ceramic Cultural Park.

FIG. 47A. OGATA KENZAN   **FIG. 47B. KITAOJI ROSANJIN**

FIG. 48. ISHIGURO MUNEMARO

FIG. 49. KAWAI KANJIRO

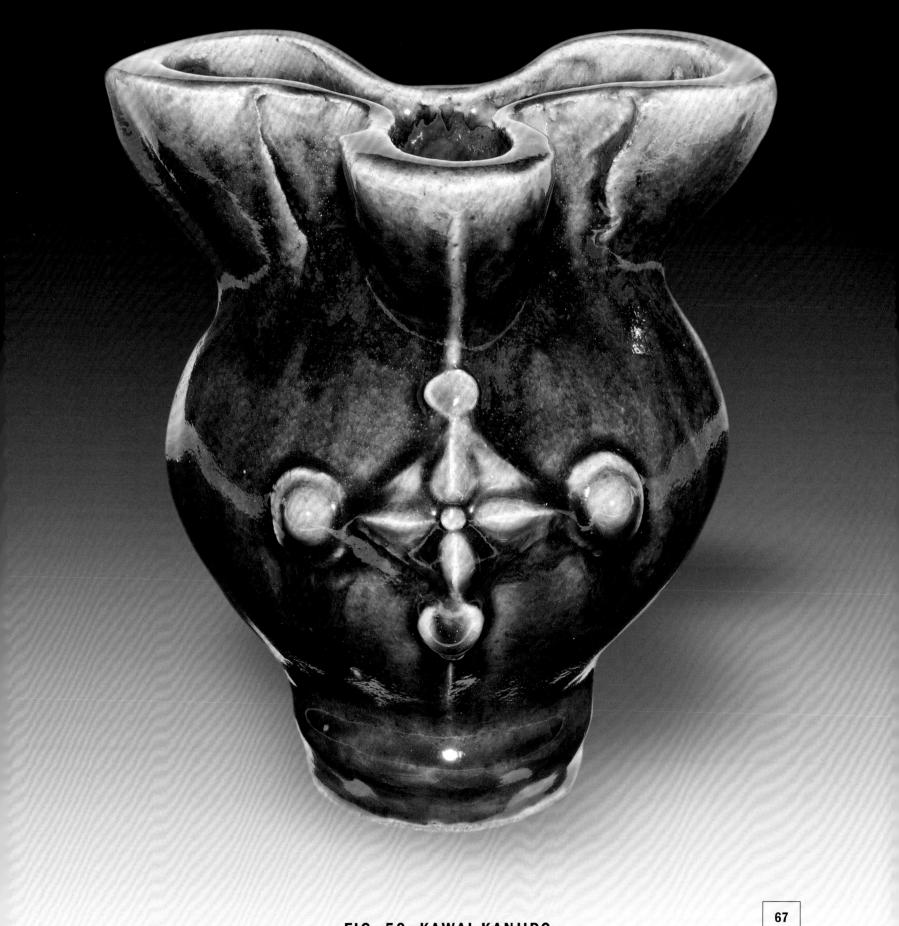

FIG. 50. KAWAI KANJIRO

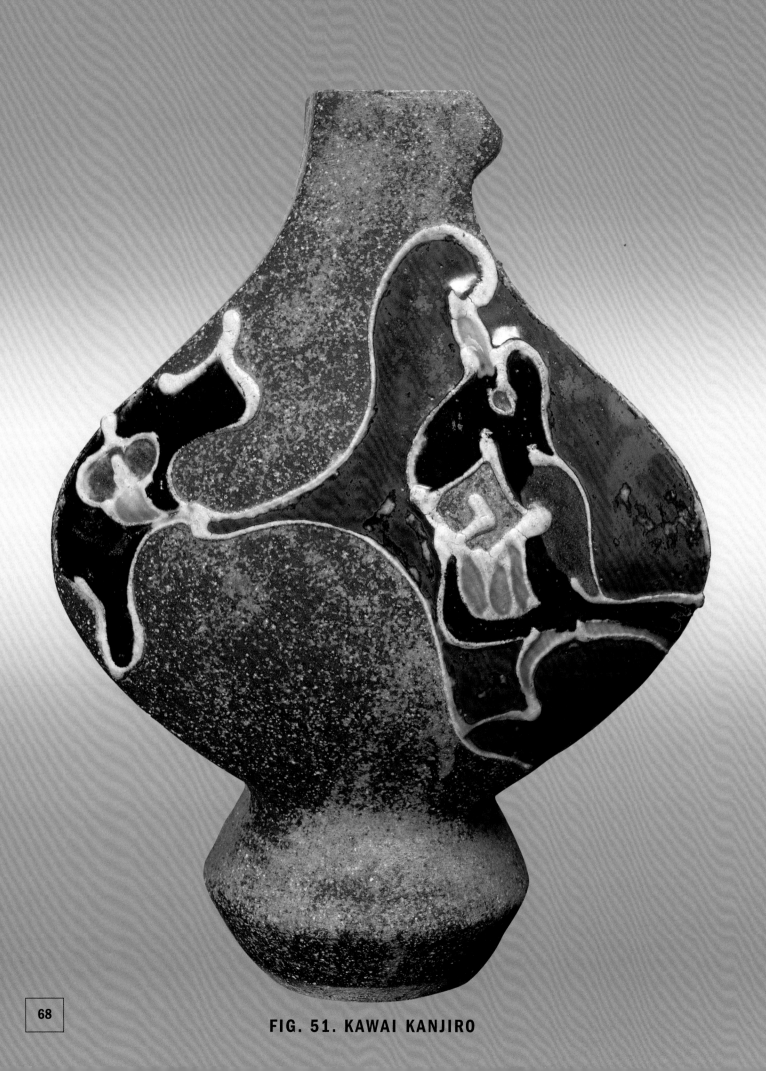

FIG. 51. KAWAI KANJIRO

FIG. 52. KAWAI KANJIRO

FIG. 53. KAWAI KANJIRO

FIG. 54. KAWAI KANJIRO

FIG. 55 TSUBOI ASUKA

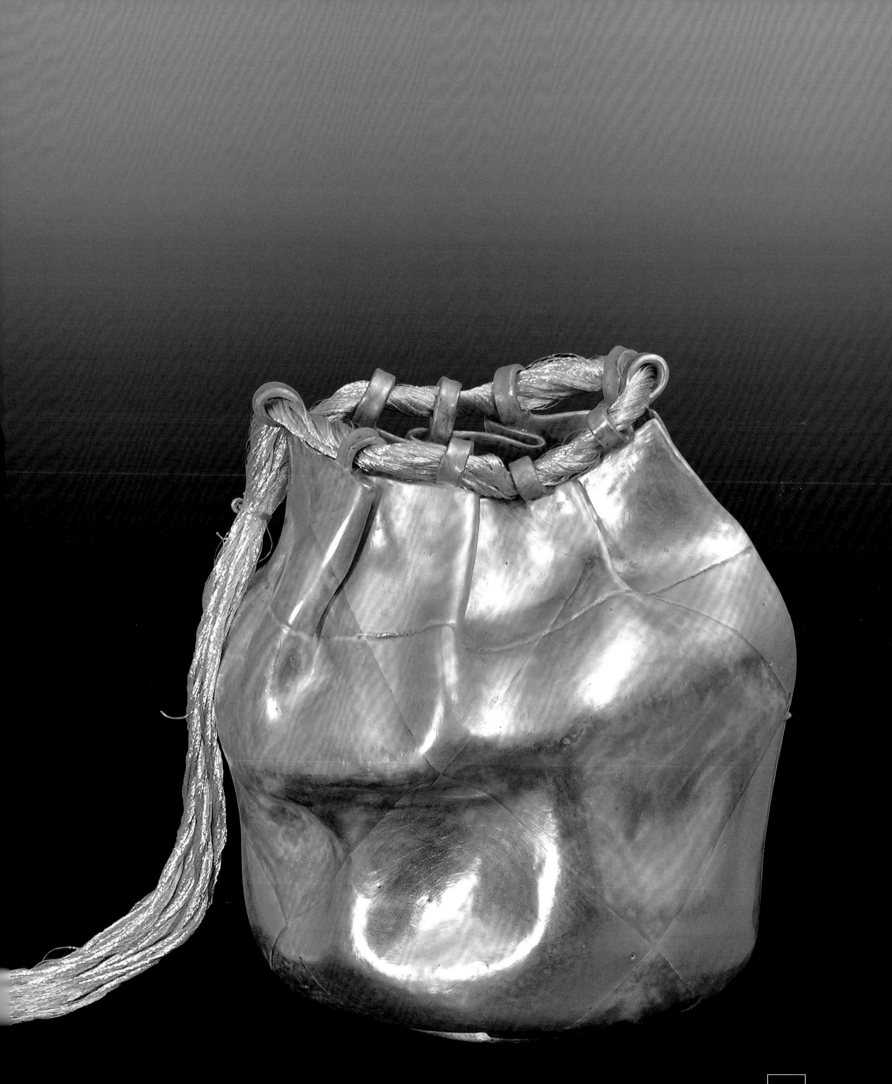

FIG. 56. TSUBOI ASUKA

FIG. 57. TSUBOI ASUKA

FIG. 58. TSUBOI ASUKA

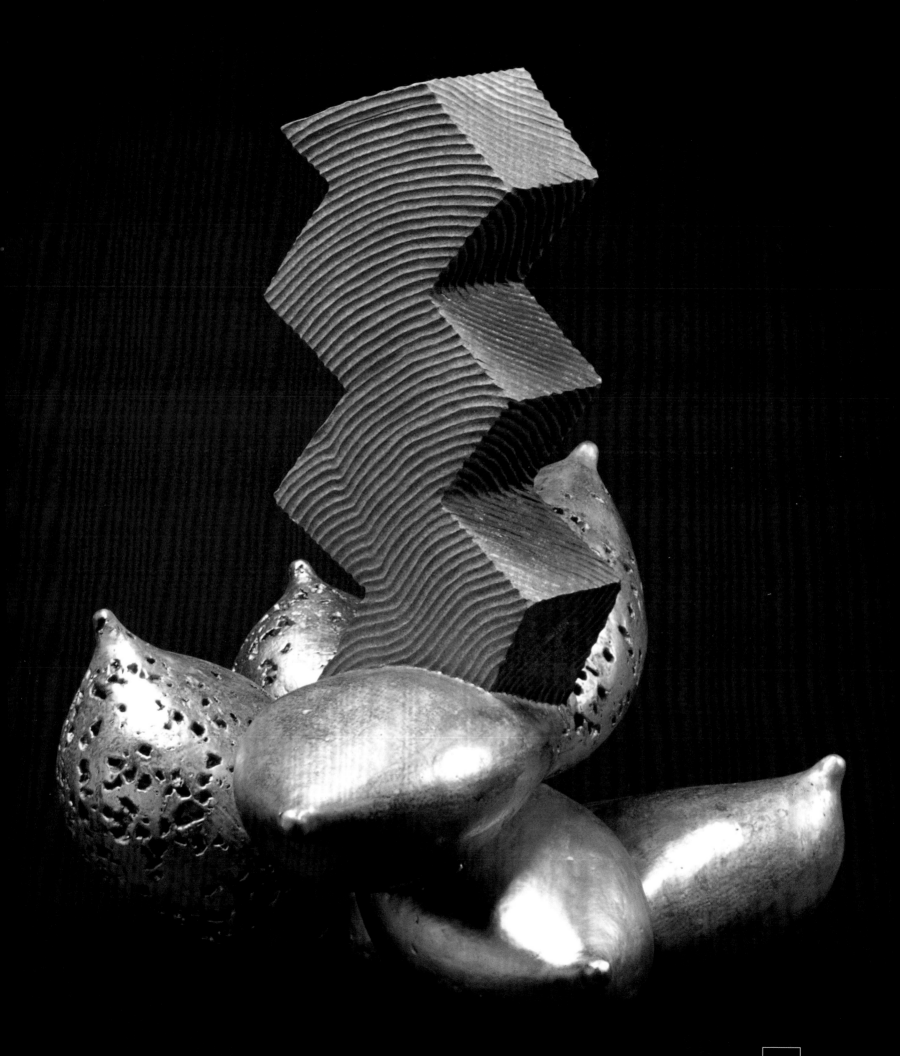

FIG. 59. TSUBOI ASUKA

FIGS. 60A, 60. FUKAMI SUEHARU

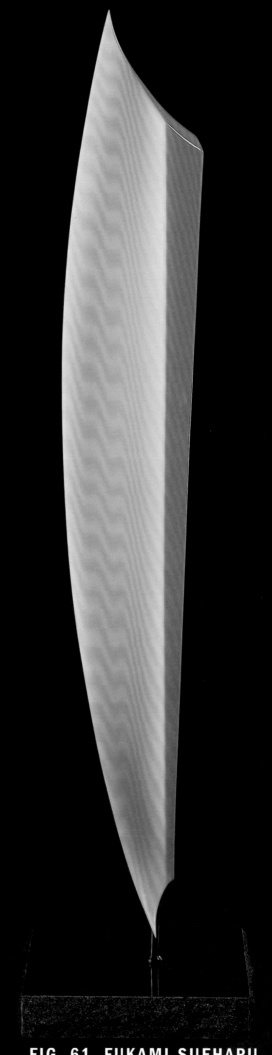

FIG. 61. FUKAMI SUEHARU

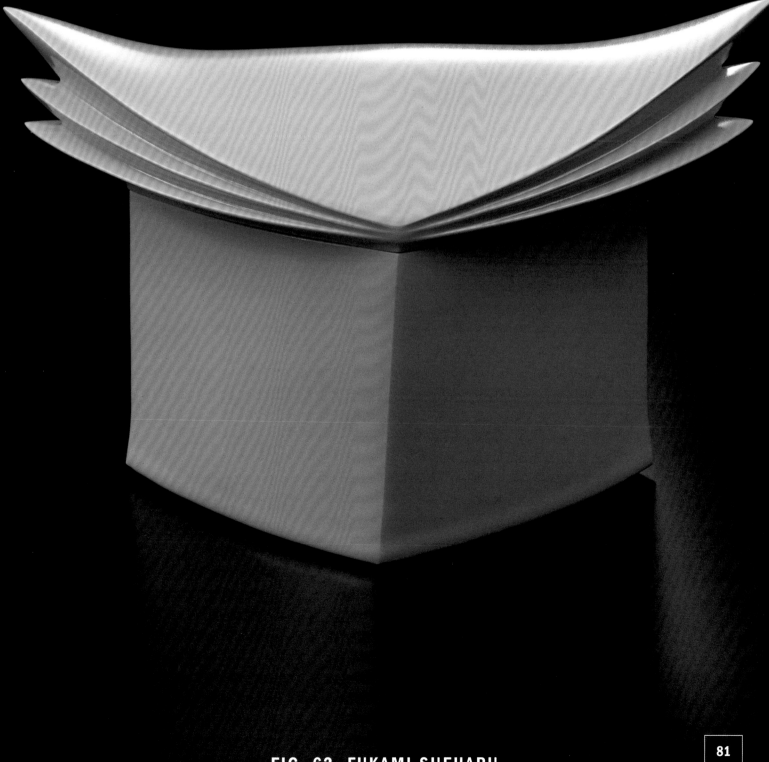

FIG. 62. FUKAMI SUEHARU

FIG. 63. TAKIGUCHI KAZUO

FIG. 64. TAKIGUCHI KAZUO

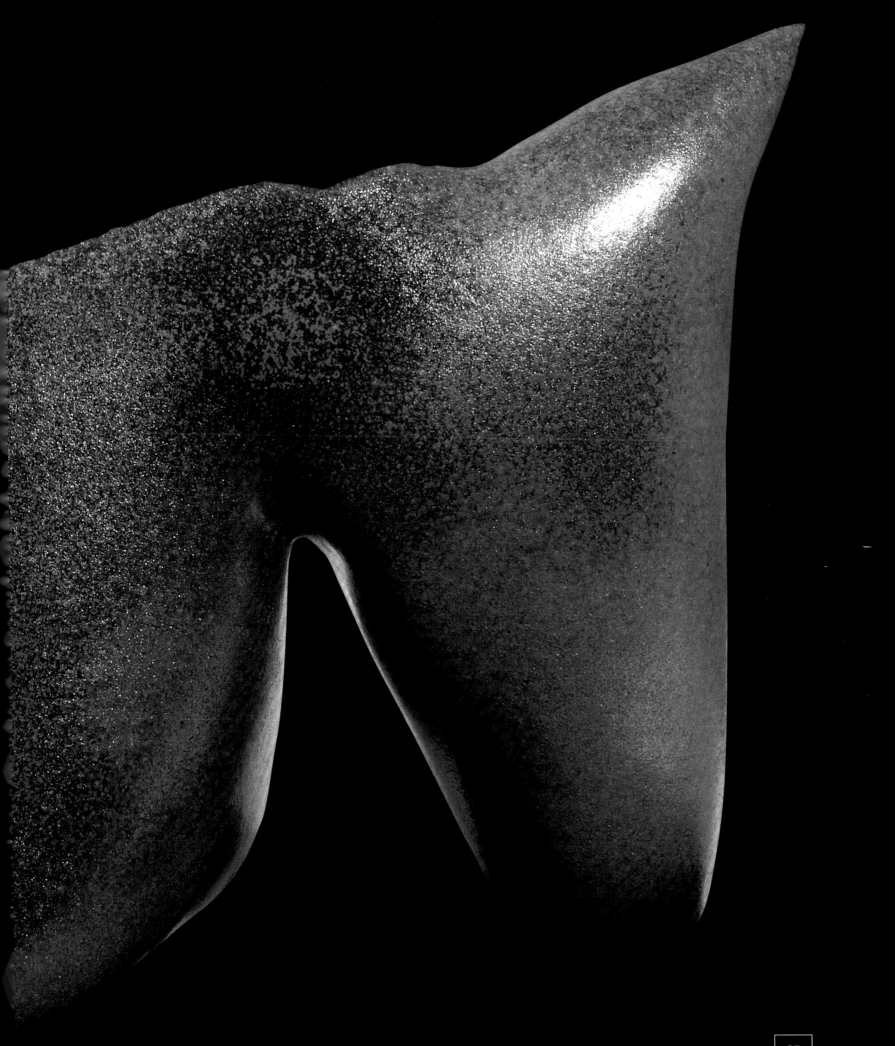

FIG. 65. TAKIGUCHI KAZUO

FIG. 66. TAKIGUCHI KAZUO

FIG. 67. HINODA TAKASHI

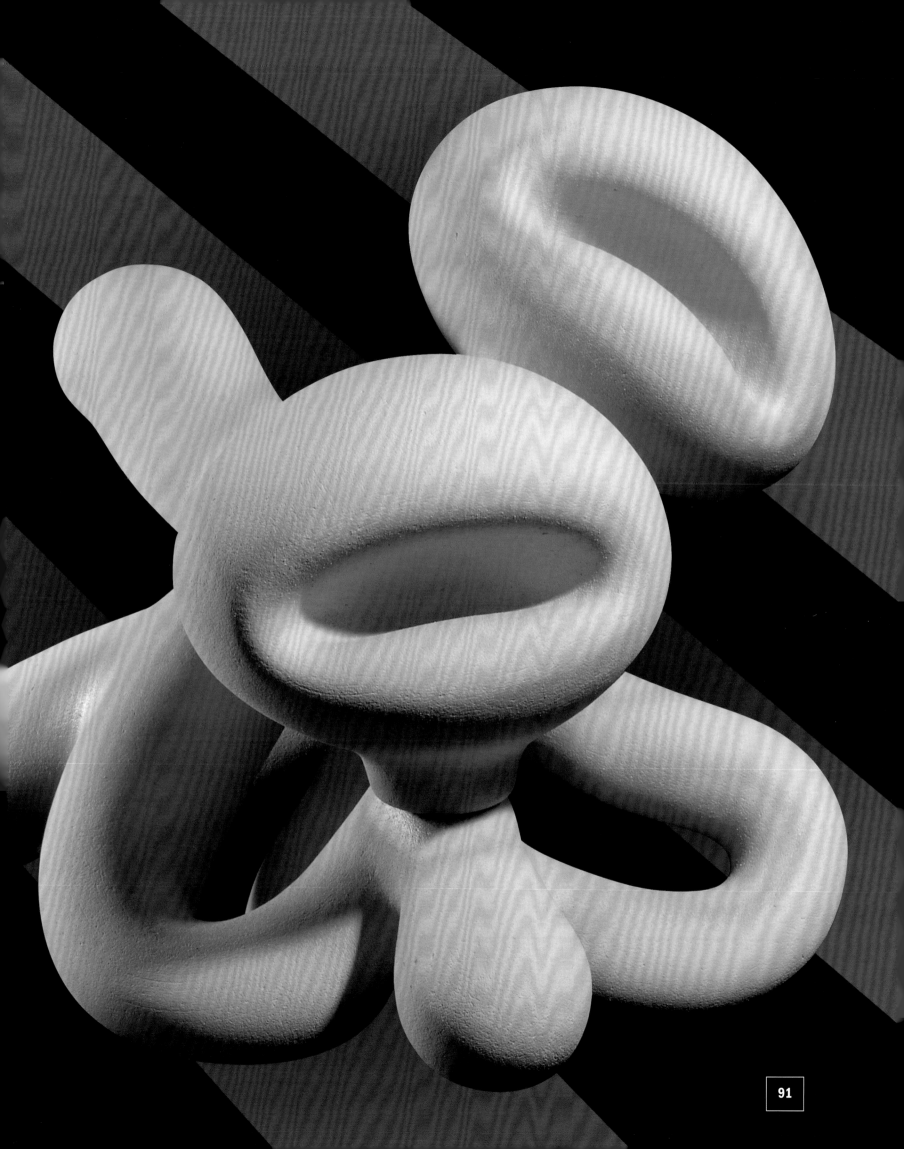

FIG. 68. HINODA TAKASHI

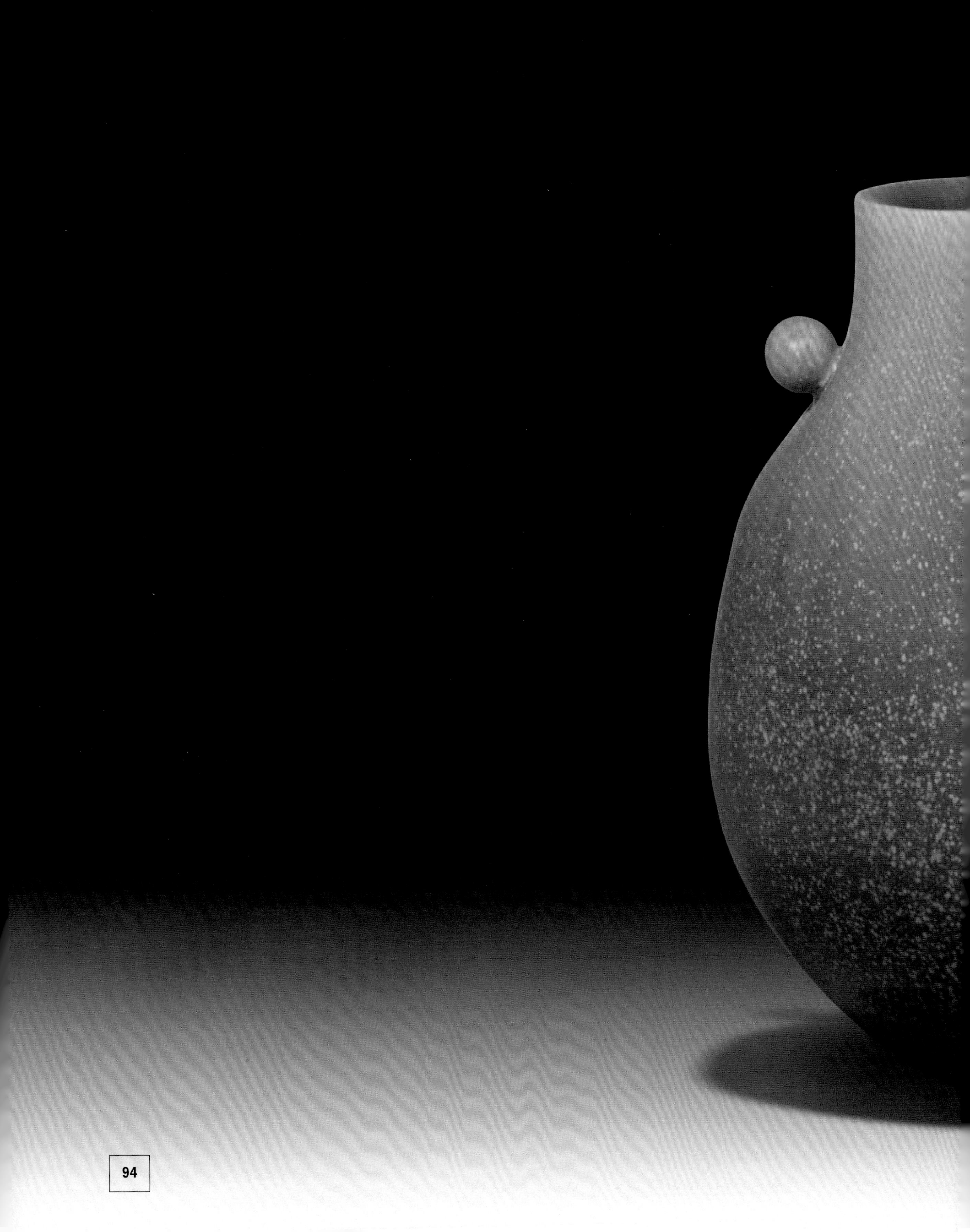

FIG. 69. YAMAZAKI AKIRA

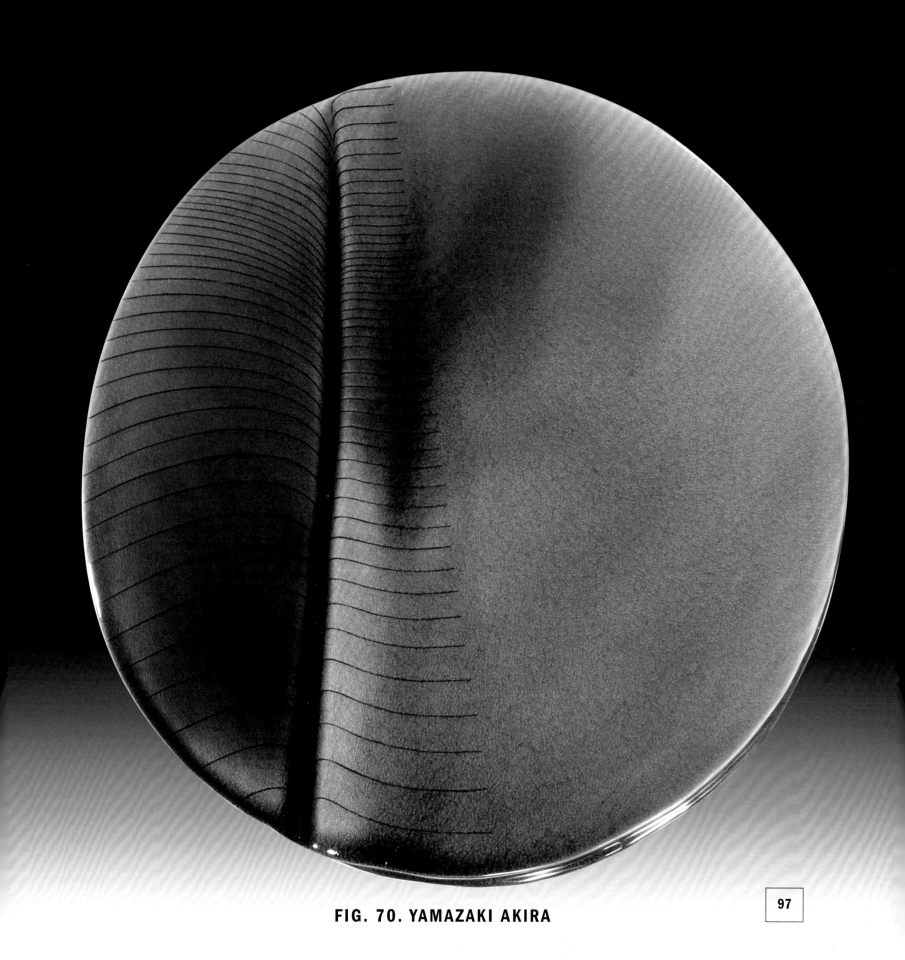

FIG. 70. YAMAZAKI AKIRA

FIG. 71. MIYASHITA ZENJI

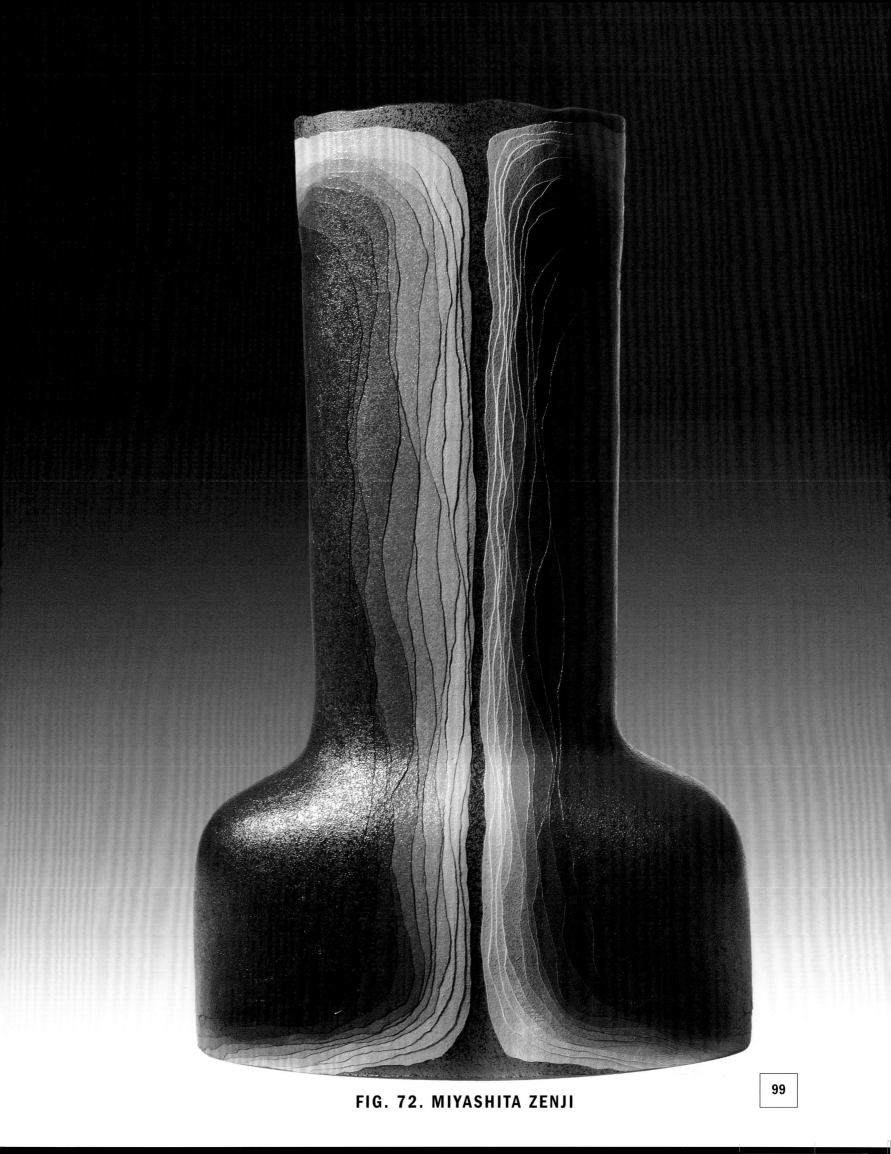

FIG. 72. MIYASHITA ZENJI

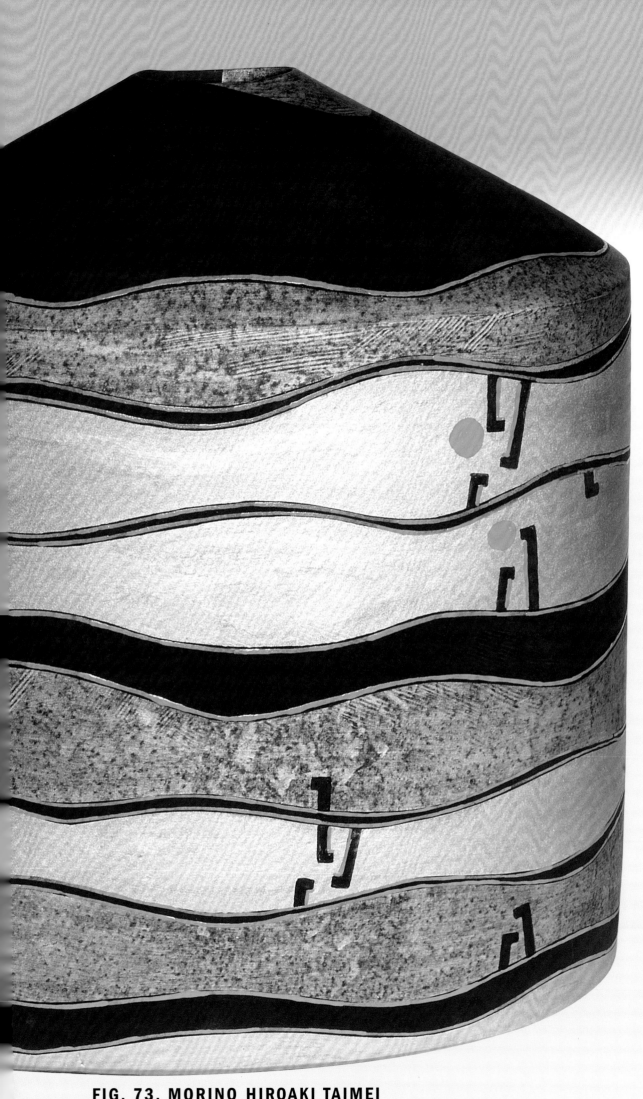

FIG. 73. MORINO HIROAKI TAIMEI

101

FIG. 74. MORINO HIROAKI TAIMEI

FIG. 75. MORINO HIROAKI TAIMEI

FIGS. 76, 77, 78.
MIYANAGA TOZAN III (RIKICHI)

105

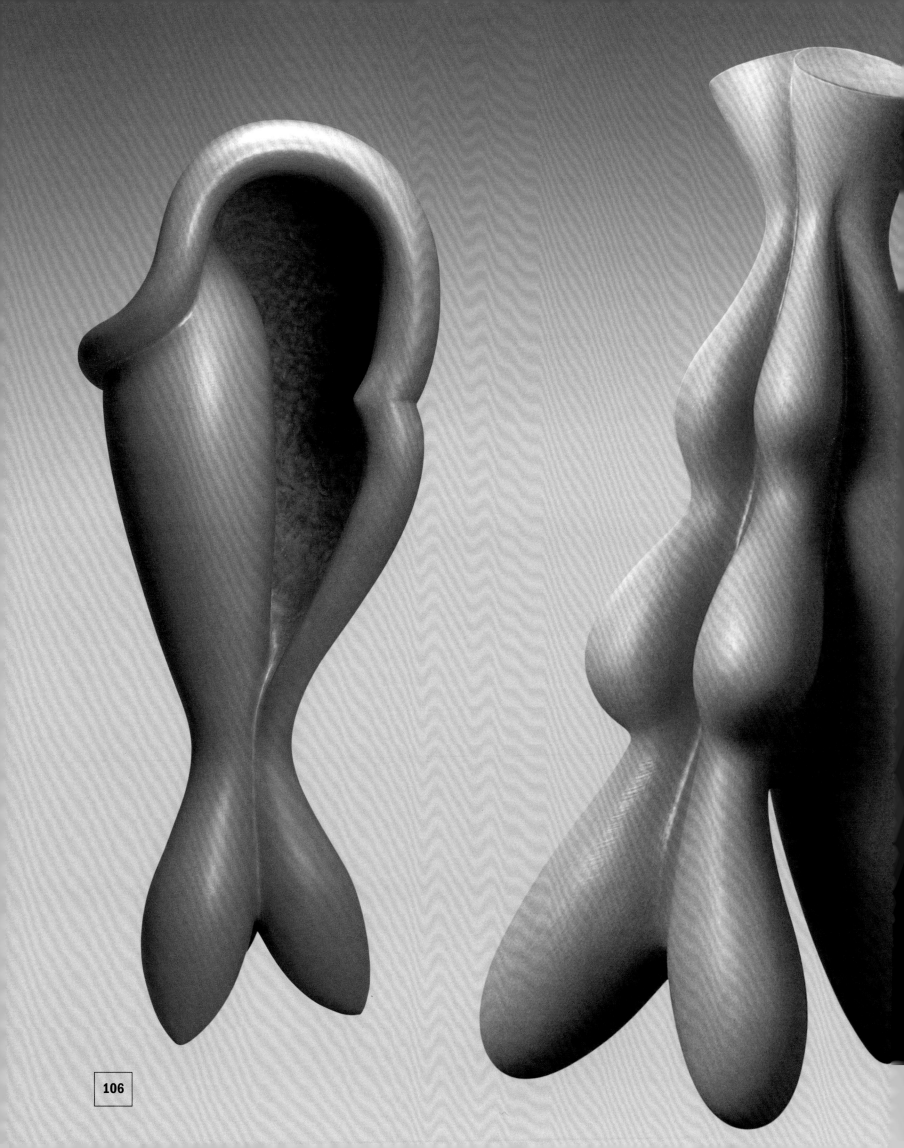

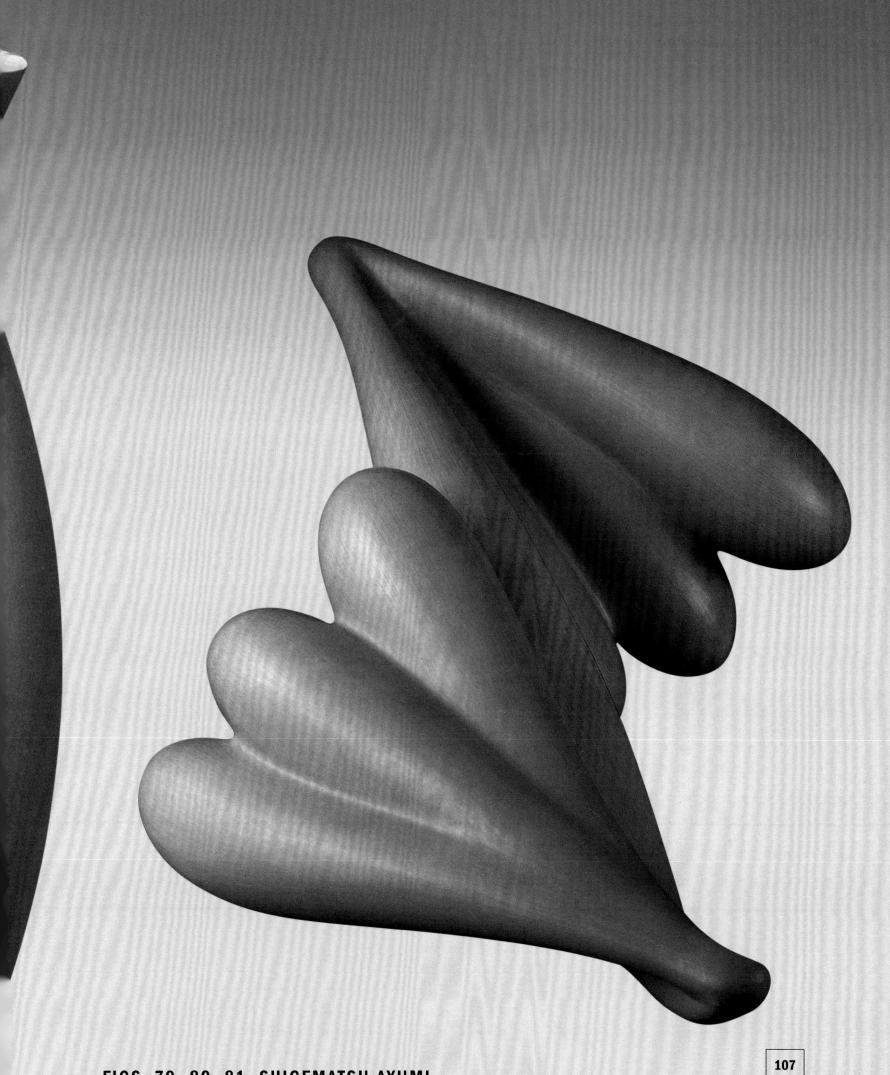

FIGS. 79, 80, 81. SHIGEMATSU AYUMI

Bizen, Shigaraki, and Iga Styles

Bizen is a remarkable town located just west of the modern city of Okayama. The correct name of the town is Imbe, but it is popularly called Bizen, which is how it is named here. A first time visitor to Bizen will be startled to discover the totality of the town's dedication to making a specific kind of pottery. A main street leads away from the train station and then branches into several directions. Almost all the businesses in operation on this street are pottery shops, one next to the other. A small museum showing old and contemporary Bizen ware is located near the train station.

The Bizen lineage can be traced back to the influence of the Sue ware of the 5th century Kofun Period. However, the first kilns in Bizen were not built until the 12th century. Its rise to prominence occurred when it's characteristic clay was seen as fittng the aesthetic requirements of tea ware during the late 16th century, the Momoyama Period. Bizen ware declined in popularity during the Edo Period, supplanted by colorful glazed ceramics. The Meiji Period saw a continuation of difficult times for Bizen. The potential for improvement started about 1935 when Kaneshige Toyo began making tea ware inspired by Momoyama Bizen pottery.

Bizen ware uses a refined, locally-produced rice field clay. It is fired at high temperatures, producing a quietly beautiful array of colors, solely as a result of the natural reaction of the clay to heat and wood ash deposits. Today in the Bizen area, there are hundreds of potters making traditionally crafted Bizen vessels. One can also find a handful of potters making ceramic sculpture using Bizen clay and traditional kilns.

Shigaraki ware is said to reach as far back as the 8th century when roofing tiles were made for the Shigaraki Palace of Emperor Shomu. Originally, because of the coarse nature of the clay, Shigaraki pottery was used primarily to store dry foods and seeds. Large Shigaraki storage jars became commonplace during the 14th century Muromachi Period. Favored by tea masters of the subsequent Momoyama Period, the popularity and esteem of Shigaraki ware soared.

Shigaraki lies in a valley between two mountains, about one hour by car from Kyoto. Unlike the pottery village of Bizen, Shigaraki boasts two outstanding museums. The Shigaraki Ceramic Cultural Park collects and exhibits ceramics from all parts of Japan, as well as internationally. The museum owns large kilns to which it invites prominent potters from all over the world to visit, to work, and to experiment.

A short drive from Shigaraki can be found one of the world's most beautiful museums, the Miho Museum, created in 1997. This private museum, owned by a religious sect, was designed by the 20th-century architect, I. M. Pei; it is surely one of his masterpieces. Upon entering the museum grounds, the visitor will feel like a pilgrim traversing the approach to the main museum exhibition building. Once inside the building, the view of the surrounding mountains is utterly memorable.

Iga is the close neighbor of Shigaraki, separated by one mountain. Its kilns were first established during the Momoyama Period. Iga ware, like Shigaraki ware, also features high-fired, unglazed work. Iga ware tends to have heavy green ash deposits from multiple firings, and to be less regular in shape than Shigaraki ware.

In traditional wood-fired kilns, clay was subject to fascinating encrustation from molten wood ash, sometimes converted into sinuous rivulets, culminating in jewel-like globules. These natural colors included jade green, mustard yellow, many shades of reds and grays, and even some blues and purples. The different inherent qualities of clay were valued: the dense fine-grained Bizen clay, free of large particles (**figs. 85, 91, 92, 96**); gritty Shigaraki clay (**figs. 82, 101–108**) and Iga clay (**figs. 84, 109, 110**), whose "impurities" activated the pots' surfaces. The final appearance of the work depended upon the inexact potter's art in selecting the type of wood to be used in the kiln, the temperature and duration of firing, the amount of oxygen, interior air currents, positioning and blockage within the kiln. As an added bonus, the kiln gods sometimes created a work which was superior to anything the potter could have devised or imagined.

Fig. 82. Shigaraki jar, Muromachi Period (14th century). This classic Shigaraki storage jar has big, brawny, powerful shoulders decorated with cross-hatching. Its rich colors and gritty surface are enhanced by golden ash.
H. 17 1/2 in. x diam. 15 in. (44.5 cm x 38.1cm). S.J. & G.W. Lurie Collection.

Fig. 83. Sue Ware, Kofun Period (250–552). Clearly composed of three parts: a long tapering neck; an oval body girded by a band of close verticals; a foot with open slots. They are united by golden wood ash in intense contrast with the blackened clay.
H. 11 in. x diam. 6 1/2 in. (27.9 cm x 16.5 cm). S.J. & G.W. Lurie Collection.

Fig. 84. Iga Ware, Momoyama Period (1568–1615). This flower vase exemplifies the unique Japanese aesthetic which recognizes that beauty can reside in distortion and imperfection. Its onion-shaped rim fits on a cylindrical, indented body, with rigid rectangular ears. The wood ash forms a jade-green glaze flowing over the red-orange surface.
H. 11 1/4 in. (28.6 cm). Tokyo National Museum.

Fig. 85. Bizen Ware, Momoyama Period (1568–1615). Robustly shaped, its beauty is realized in a very contemporary way, exposing the process of its making on a potter's wheel by not smoothing over the prominent horizontal lines.
H. 13 1/2 in. x diam. 12 1/2 in. (34.3 cm x 31.7cm). S.J. & G.W. Lurie Collection.

110

FIG. 82. MUROMACHI PERIOD   FIG. 83. KOFUN PERIOD

FIGS. 84, 85. MOMOYAMA PERIOD

Bizen Artists

Kaneshige Toyo
(1896–1967)

Regarded as the father of modern Bizen ware, in the 1930s Kaneshige Toyo made a close study of Momoyama Bizen pottery in private collections, and of old Bizen pottery fragments and kilns. This led him to create work in his own style, inspired by Momoyama Bizen ware, which ultimately revitalized the great Bizen tradition. By his example and under his influence, Bizen potters changed their concentration to tea ceramic utensils, vases and table ware. Before Kaneshige, Bizen potters, including his own father, chiefly made Okimono, small clay animal figures. In 1956, Kaneshige Toyo was appointed a Living National Treasure for his outstanding Bizen work and for his important contribution to reviving the great Bizen ceramic tradition.

Figs. 86, 87. 1963. Kaneshige's two tea ceremony water jars embody rich, colorful firing effects. Sturdily constructed, they find glory in a solid union with the great Bizen heritage.

H. 8 in. (20 cm). Tokyo National Museum of Modern Art.
H. 7 1/4 in. (18.4 cm). Toyo Kaneshige Kinenkan.

Fig. 88. 1954. This ceremony flower vase exhibits warm glowing colors and sensitively placed marks that add vitality to the body. It is illustrated here against a background detail from figure 86.

H. 9 3/4 in. x diam. 5 in. (24.8 cm x 12.7 cm). Toyo Kaneshige Kinenkan.

Fujiwara Kei
(1899–1983)

Fujiwara Kei, who came to pottery late after devoting himself to literature, was another important figure in re-establishing the prestige of the Bizen tradition. Unlike Kaneshige Toyo, who re-created Momoyama glory, Fujiwara Kei's inspiration was focused on earlier periods, Kamakura (1185-1333) and Muromachi (1333-1568). Thus, Fujiwara Kei's work is generally tougher, simpler and more direct. He was designated a Living National Treasure in 1970.

Fig. 89. The dark brown, reddish and mustard lava-like wood ash glazes flow downward from the rim. This piece compels attention with its raw, forceful directness.

Private collection.

Fig. 90. Fujiwara Kei's massive, scorched and blackened vessel. Like a cannonball set on a high perforated foot, it exudes a no-nonsense power. It is lightened by misty gold and a crescent of gray wood ash deposits on its shoulder. The incised calligraphy on this piece reads "Dream," here a dark nightmare activity.

Private collection.

Fujiwara Yu
(1933–2001)

Fujiwara Yu, the son of Fujiwara Kei, was designated a Living National Treasure in 1996. Although he traveled extensively in Europe and the U.S.A., he never fell under the spell of Western art. To those privileged to watch Yu throw pots, the experience was unforgettable. Yu's self-confidence, speed and perfect craftsmanship were astonishing. The Fujiwara compound, large, impressive and overlooking the inland sea of Japan, served as the home, studio, museum and cemetery for the Fujiwara family. Their private museum, open to the public, contains the work of father and son, as well as ancient Bizen ware.

Figs. 91, 92. c. 1980. The early pioneers in reviving traditional Bizen ware have been followed by hundreds of contemporary Bizen potters. Prominent among them is Fujiwara Yu, notable for his quiet, elegant, subtly colored vessels. His work is a definitive example of classic modern Bizen art, faultless in form and execution, more affecting for being understated. Fujiwara Yu's oeuvre manifests his confidence that modest unadorned pottery can achieve great things. He makes no attempt to disguise his phenomenal craftsmanship, nor his reliance on simple forms uncorrupted by deliberate deformations. His is a world of clear, clean, balanced, fine, highly sophisticated, pleasurable vessels.

Fig. 91. H. 10 3/4 in. x diam. 3 7/8 in. (27.3 cm x 9.8 cm). S.J. & G.W. Lurie Collection.

Fig. 92. H. 10 3/4 in. x diam. 10 1/2 in. (27.3 cm x 26.6 cm). S.J. & G.W. Lurie Collection.

Kaneshige Kosuke
(b. 1943)

Kaneshige Kosuke, a son of Toyo, the first Living National Treasure from Bizen, has made an independent adjustment to his family pottery heritage, which can be traced back as far as 15th-century Bizen. Kosuke uses the same Bizen clay and the same type traditional kiln that his father used. Some of his pieces retain a barely discernible vestige, a small top opening, of the vessel form. However, at this point the forms of his work show the result of his training as a sculptor at the Tokyo National University of Arts & Music. Kosuke has developed his own vocabulary of resonant sculptural forms.

P xvi. *Birth of Kings*, 1991. Shaped like a head, faintly militaristic, it lies painfully on a construction of torturous stakes. Kosuke here deals with themes of power, danger, pain, and struggle. This work is a comment on the employment of the fear, menace and cruel punishment necessary to attain and retain royal power. The title says it all.

H.18 in. x w. 13 in. x d. 13 in. (45.7 cm x 33 cm x 33 cm). Private collection.

Fig. 93. *Saint's Garment*, c. 2000. Starting with a conventional diamond-shaped vase, Kosuke then carefully arranged slabs of clay around the form, creating voluptuous folds. When seen in the round, one can appreciate the beautiful complexity of the clay drapery: a variety of light and shaded areas; shapes that appear stable and others that are about to fall. The delicate parallel combed lines of the surfaces play against the luxuriant folds. Kosuke has achieved an exciting transformation by raising the banal image of textile to a monumental sculpture.

H. 15 1/4 in. x w. 16 in. x l. 20 in. (38.7 cm x 40.6 cm x 50.8 cm). S.J. & G.W. Lurie Collection.

Fig. 94. *From the Sea*, c. 2000. At a glance, we know that something momentous has occurred, compelling a close examination. This sunken warship, with ominous projections, whose incised hull armor is intact, has been violently twisted by an unidentified disastrous force. Numerous loose, long planks or beams, sometimes suggesting one-eyed fish, show the utter destruction of the ship's top deck. Its center is empty. The tough armor, even though it held together, failed to prevent this catastrophe. This wrecked warship tells us that both inner and outer strength are necessary for survival.

H. 15 1/2 in. x w. 13 3/4 in. x d. 15 in. (39.3 cm x 34.9 cm. x 38.1 cm). S.J. & G.W. Lurie Collection.

Fig. 95. A detail of *From the Sea* series.

Toyofuku Hiroshi

Some years ago, this potter participated in a group show at a major Tokyo department store art gallery. His exhibition lasted no more than six days. The vase illustrated is an example of the best work produced by the hundreds of active Bizen potters whose names and works are all but unknown to general pottery lovers.

Fig. 96. 1982. Sometimes less is more. This one-stem flower vase succeeds by the least complicated means. A single rice straw has been wrapped around the wet clay body, placed in a protected box to avoid fallen ash, and fired in the kiln. The heat of the kiln burned away the straw, leaving a weaving red residue on the neck and body—minimal, sufficient and quite perfect.

H. 11 in. x diam. 7 in. (27.9 cm x 17.7 cm). S.J. & G.W. Lurie Collection.

Abe Anjin
(b. 1938)

At the age of 34, Abe Anjin, then chiefly active as a painter, had a near-death experience from illness and decided to be re-born, as it were, as a potter and sculptor. He is particularly successful in making Ko-Bizen (old Bizen) style tea ware that has an authentic ancient feeling, while avoiding mere copying of Momoyama Bizen ware.

Fig. 97. 1995. Illustrated here is a powerfully built example of Abe's Momoyama-type Bizen water jars with especially vigorous incisions and grooves gouged into the brown and gold rugged body.

H. 8 1/2 in. x diam. 9 1/2 in. (21.6 cm x 24.1 cm). S.J. & G.W. Lurie Collection.

Yamamoto Izuru
(b. 1944)

Yamamoto Izuru has worked under the difficult circumstances of being the fourth son of a Bizen ceramist who was named a Living National Treasure and, to make matters still more trying, as the younger brother of another Bizen ceramist who has been named an Okayama Prefecture Living National Treasure. Yamamoto studied Western sculpture in Japan and then in Paris, yet when he came back to Japan, he realized, as he put it, that clay was in his blood. From his western training he absorbed a respect for the dynamic and was encouraged to explore adventurous forms. His eastern heritage is responsible for the quiet, unhurried spirit of his work and his continued use of a traditional wood-fired kiln. His finest works have dazzling effects of light, shadow and surface texture on layered forms. The works here are the final result of Yamamoto's painstaking method of stacking and cutting specially prepared layers of thin clay.

Fig. 98. *Vase in Ginko-leaf Shape*, 2005; **Fig. 99.** *Progressive Change*, 2005. These two pieces complement each other perfectly. One is in the process of gradually opening up or expanding; the other is in the process of closing. The closing piece has a stacked layered body. Long, sensitive fingers are slowly encroaching on the remaining open area. We are witnesses to the drama of the last moments before the opening is engulfed. The edges of the wave-like layers shimmer in captured light. The companion piece, a Ginko leaf shape is a friendlier, graceful work, whose surface dances in the light.

H. 17 in. x w. 17 1/2 in. x d. 5 1/2 in. (43.2 cm x 44.5 cm x 14 cm). Private collection.

H. 17 in. x w. 14 in. x d. 9 in. (43.2 cm x 35.5 x 22.8 cm). S.J. & G.W. Lurie Collection.

Fig. 100. *Embracing*, 2006. Aptly named, two massive, layered clay waves with rusticated surfaces intertwine, becoming a unity. This work is a triumphant expression of what a superb artist can do to vitalize a basic vessel form. Emerging from a narrow base, gathering strength and volume as they rise, are two living forces of oceanic power.

Shown here are three views of the same piece.

H. 23 1/2 in. x w. 18 in. x d. 11 in. (59.7 cm x 45.7 cm x 28 cm). S.J. & G.W. Lurie Collection.

FIG. 86. KANESHIGE TOYO

FIG. 87. KANESHIGE TOYO

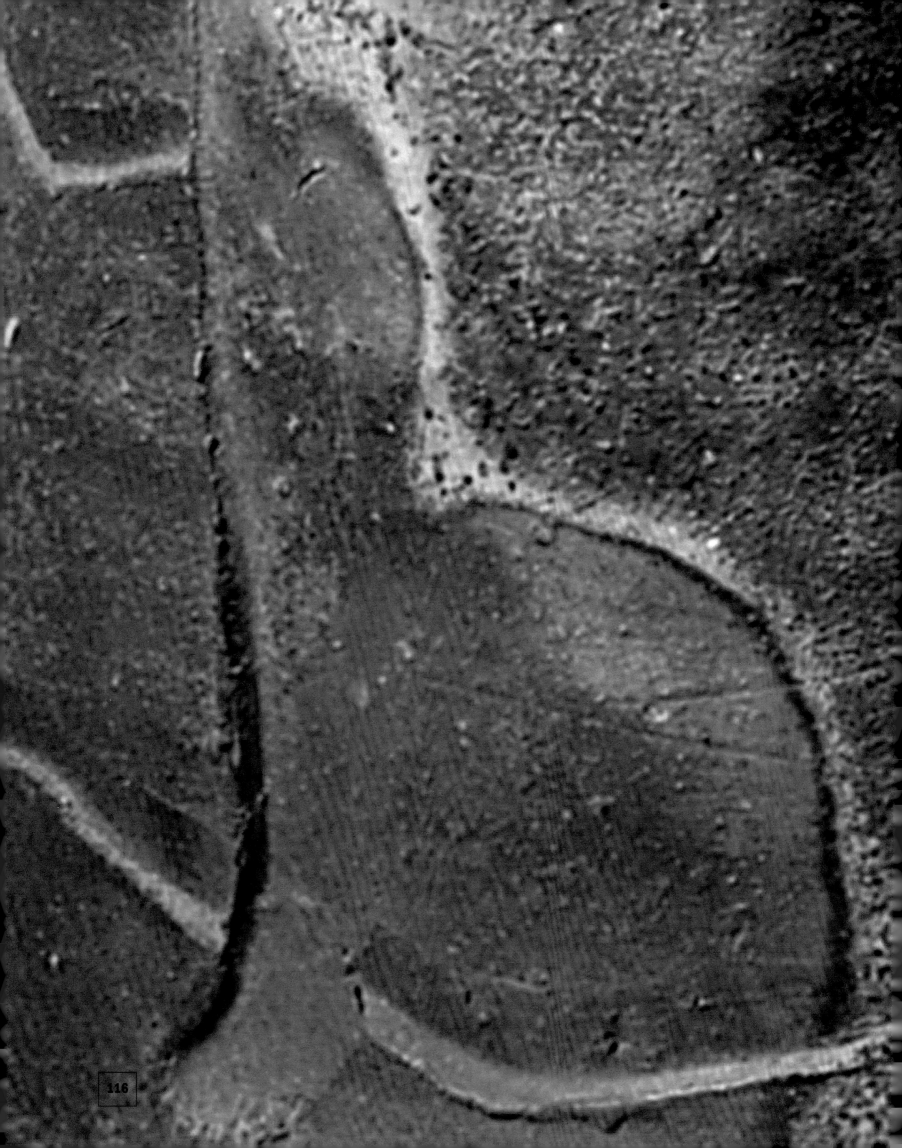

116

FIG. 88. KANESHIGE TOYO

117

FIG. 89. FUJIWARA KEI

FIG. 90. FUJIWARA KEI

120

FIG. 91. FUJIWARA YU

FIG. 92. FUJIWARA YU

FIG. 93. KANESHIGE KOSUKE

FIG. 94. KANESHIGE KOSUKE

125

FIG. 95. KANESHIGE KOSUKE

FIG. 96. TOYOFUKU HIROSHI

129

FIG. 97. ABE ANJIN

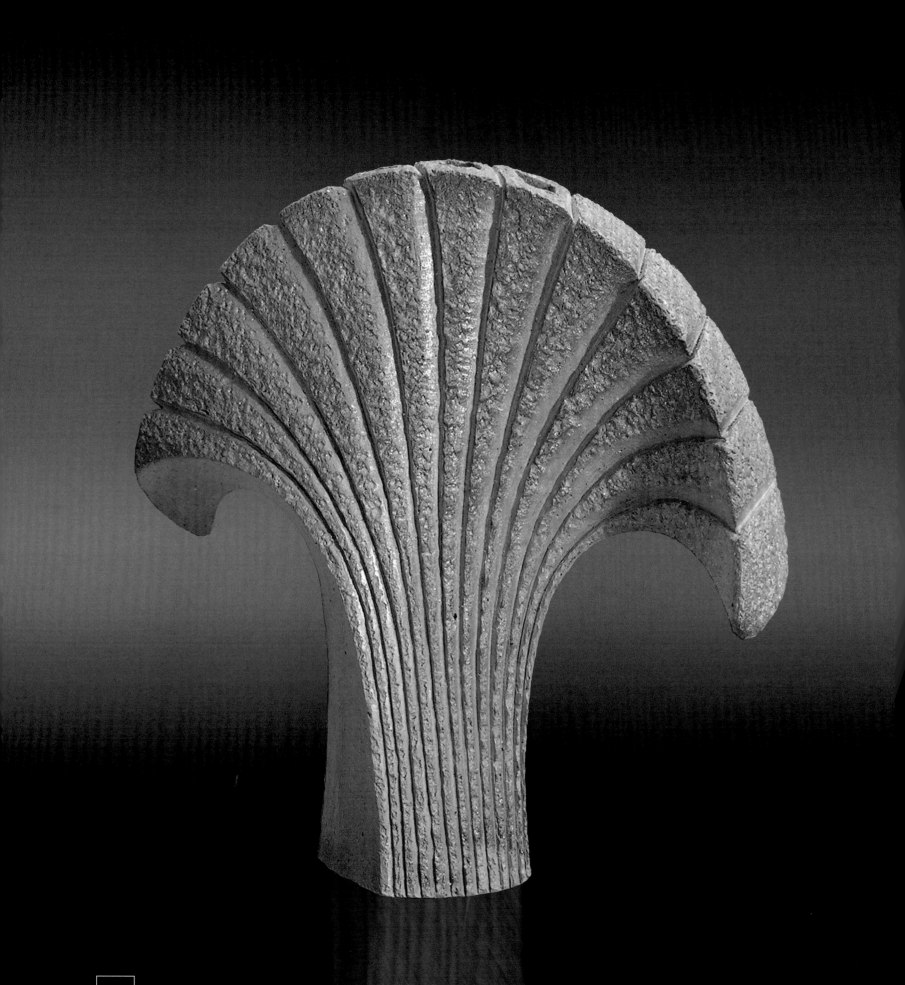

FIG. 98. YAMAMOTO IZURU

FIG. 99. YAMAMOTO IZURU

FIG. 100. YAMAMOTO IZURU

Shigaraki and Iga Artists

Kohara Yasuhiro
(b. 1954)

Kohara is an unusual combination of an artist essentially following the great Shigaraki tradition, whose personal lifestyle is untraditional. Kohara loves music, particularly jazz, drives a red European sports car, loves scuba diving and enjoys dining at exquisite restaurants. This artist never studied with a master or at a ceramic school. He is entirely self-taught. It is unsurprising that out of this unusual background, Kohara has given us Shigaraki ceramics with a distinct personal and unconventional twist.

Fig. 101. The rugged beauty of this large basket includes its high razor-sharp walls and a powerful jagged strap handle (not clearly shown on this photo). The walls, composed of gritty Shigaraki clay covered with wood ash glaze, are so formidable that they suggest a fortress. This monumental presence could be dramatically heightened by the placement of a single delicate flower.

H. 27 in. x w. 41 in. (69 cm x 104 cm). Private Collection, California.

Fig. 102. 2005. Natural wood ash glaze has always been considered an essential characteristic of Shigaraki ware. Kohara, who loves those natural effects, has, nevertheless, questioned the traditional view that all of the color must be the result only of heat, clay and wood ash. This broad rim is an excellent example of the natural glaze produced by wood ash. However, Kohara has painted the center and then fired it, challenging tradition. Ever ready to question orthodoxy, Kohara asks why should there be a wall between a painted surface and a wood ash glaze surface as a matter of untested principle? Like the jazz musicians he admires, he is ready to improvise, to add his own grace note to the traditional melody of Shigaraki. Kohara makes no attempt to mislead or falsify what he has done. The result is startling. There is an exciting contrast between the surface texture, color and design of the painted center, and the very different rim surface. Kohara's anti-traditional combination has opened up interesting creative possibilities.

H. 4 1/2 in. x diam. 17 3/4 in. (11.4 cm x 45 cm). Private collection.

Fig. 103. 2003. The exciting rivulets of natural green wood ash glaze, culminating in "dragonfly eye" globules, are prized by connoisseurs. The rough, rustic quality invites the company of delicate flowers.

H. 10 in. x diam. 5 1/2 in. (25.4 cm x 13.9 cm). S.J. & G.W. Lurie Collection.

Koyama Yasuhisa
(b. 1936)

Koyama Yasuhisa occupies a rare place in contemporary Japanese ceramics. He is among the few potters who have managed to retain a close identification with traditional pottery and, at the same time, produce a high level of imaginative work. All of Koyama's pieces are made from grainy Shigaraki clay, are fired in traditional kilns and are colored only by natural wood ash deposits. Each of his pieces will accept functional use as a flower vase. Up to this point, it is not possible to be more traditional. But, as his work demonstrates, Koyama's acute creative sensibility has expanded and revitalized the possibilities of Shigaraki ceramics. He may be the most sculpturally adventurous of all of the Shigaraki potters.

Fig. 104 is a detail of **Fig. 105** which focuses on the contrasts of surface textures.

Fig. 105. 1995. Koyama gives us a glowing vessel, whose arms are raised upwards like those of an ecstatic dancer or as in fervent prayer. The work is a study in contrasts. The outer edges are torn and jagged, the inner edges are smooth; one side of the vessel is smooth and the other side has a rough texture.

H. 22 1/4 in. x w. 19 1/2 in. (56.5 cm x 49.5 cm). S.J. & G.W. Lurie Collection.

Fig. 106. 1990. Koyama starts with the most banal form for a flower vase—a basic cylinder. That cylinder is embraced and partially enveloped by a protective, sheltering, over-sized, looming—or Buddhist cobra-like—hood, which becomes a memorable backdrop. The surface of both the cylinder and the backdrop are highlighted by comb markings, a reference to ancient pottery. The pinched edges of the hood have a rapid improvised quality.

H. 23 1/4 in. x w. 10 in. x diam. 4 1/4 in. (59.1 cm x 4 cm x 10.7 cm). S.J. & G.W. Lurie Collection.

Fig. 107. 1999. A dazzling, monumental high column is as much an example of architecture in miniature as ceramic sculpture. Koyama used a wire tool to create a surface of striated animation. The lower one-third is decisively separated from the top portion by a large, carved-out section.

H. 23 1/4 in. x w. 4 3/4 in. (59.1 cm x 12 cm). S.J. & G.W. Lurie Collection.

Fig. 108. 1997. An ordinary vessel is transformed into a fascinating multi-faceted sculpture. Smooth is opposed by rough; lighter versus darker; geometry adjacent to irregularity. These are four views of the same piece.

H. 11 3/4 in. (29.8 cm). S.J. & G.W. Lurie Collection.

Sugimoto Sadamitsu
(b. 1935)

Sugimoto Sadamitsu is a leading Iga potter, who has acted as sensei, or teacher, for other potters. Sugimoto himself is a quiet, modest, very private person—traits that were probably enhanced when he studied in 1947 under a Zen master at the celebrated Daitoku-ji Temple, Kyoto. His serious approach to ceramics is reflected in the fact that he mostly produces tea ceremony utensils. But modesty of character does not mean that his pieces will be quiet and reserved. On the contrary, his work shows a zest for color and dramatic texture. Sugimoto welcomed both the inwardly directed practice of Zen, as well as the outward reach of a keen social conscience. He devotes considerable time with Down's Syndrome children making ceramics.

Fig. 109. c. 1990; **Fig. 110.** c. 2000. Sugimoto's water jar and flower vase exhibit vivid streaked gray areas, which contrast with the green ash and orange-red clay bodies. The continuing vitality and appeal of the Iga tradition is evident.

Fig. 109. H. 6 1/4 in. x diam. 8 3/4 in. (15.8 cm x 22 cm). Private collection.

Fig. 110. H.10 1/2 in. x diam. 5 1/4 in. (26.7 x 13.3 cm). S.J. & G.W. Lurie Collection

FIG 101. KOHARA YASUHIRO

FIG. 102. KOHARA YASUHIRO

FIG. 103. KOHARA YASUHIRO

137

138

FIG. 104. KOYAMA YASUHISA

FIG. 105. KOYAMA YASUHISA

FIG. 106. KOYAMA YASUHISA

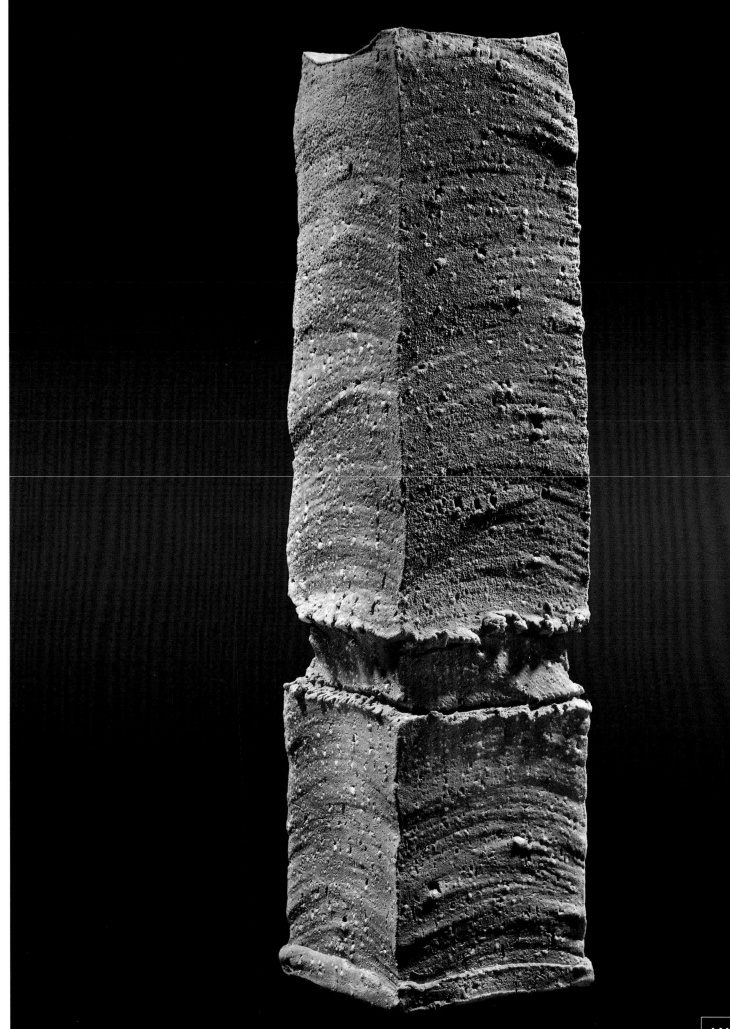

FIG. 107. KOYAMA YASUHISA

FIG. 108. KOYAMA YASUHISA

144

FIG. 109. SUGIMOTO SADAMITSU

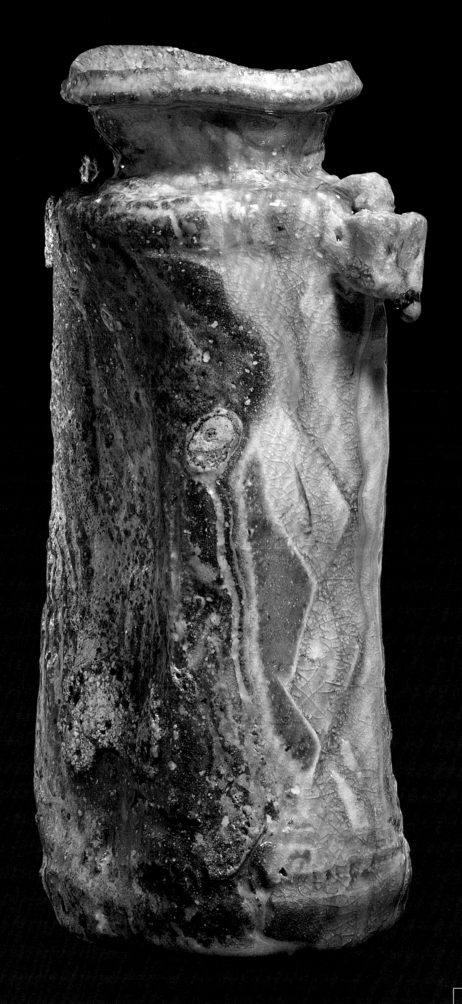

FIG. 110. SUGIMOTO SADAMITSU

Oribe Style

FIG. 111. MOMOYAMA PERIOD
FIG. 112. MOMOYAMA PERIOD

Oribe ceramics are usually characterized by a special, unmistakable deep-green glaze. In order to understand today's Oribe practitioners, it is useful to remember that it is named after a famous Tea Master, Furuta Oribe, and began during the Momoyama Period as an avant-garde response to the ceramics that had been fashionable for the tea ceremony. Momoyama ceramists working in the Oribe style produced unexpected and unprecedented asymmetrical shapes, often quite whimsical, and shocking color combinations of orange and green, and white and black. This quirky, youthful Oribe approach to ceramics continues today. The three Oribe artists illustrated below share that essential Oribe spirit, while searching for new variations and arriving at very different solutions.

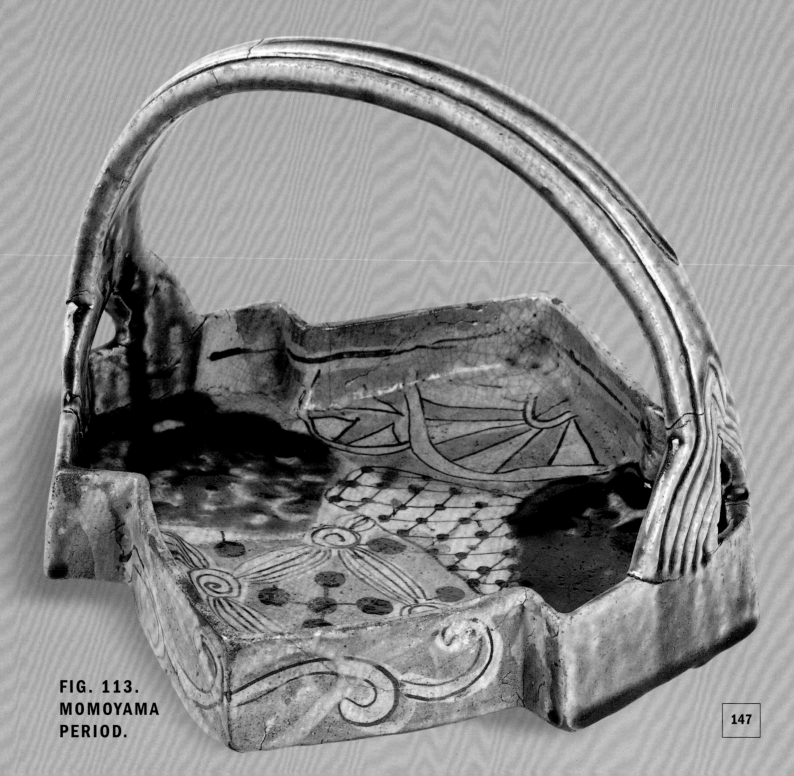

FIG. 113. MOMOYAMA PERIOD.

147

Oribe Style

Fig. 111. Momoyama Period (1568–1603). These three Oribe cups are notable for their uncomplicated gaiety and simple design motifs that appeal to the contemporary eye.
H. 4 in. (10.1 cm). Suntory Museum of Art.

Figs. 112, 113. Momoyama Period (1568–1603). The rectangular box and the tray with a handle share the basic Oribe design, color and spirit exemplified by doodles, geometrics and batches of color. These may have been declarations of artistic independence, even impudence, instances where a strong art trend led the way in a struggle against all things rigid, humorless, stiflingly serious and suffering from doctrinaire rigor mortis.
Fig. 112. H. 3 5/8 in. x w. 7 7/8 in. x d. 7 1/8 in. (9.2 cm x 20 cm x 18cm). Suntory Museum of Art.

Fig. 113. H. 7 1/16 in. x 10 3/4 in. (17.7 cm x 26.8 cm). Kitamura Museum.

Higashida Shigemasa
(b. 1955)
Higashida turned to ceramics after a brief but successful career as a stock trader at a major brokerage firm. Ceramic school and an apprenticeship with a master potter followed. Now fully committed to ceramic art, Higashida has stored a lifetime supply of a special clay he prefers.

Although Higashida works in both the Shino and Oribe styles, his preeminent success has been in his Oribe work. He can be seen, quite simply, as an incomparable landscape artist. Verdant green mountains; blue waterfalls, white with foam; crystalline blue lakes; dramatic ridges overlooking valleys—all are characteristics of his best Oribe work.

Fig. 114. 2000. In this miraculous platter, we see lakes of blue water, mustard yellow and deep green jagged heights, rising next to smooth, low-lying fields. Layer upon layer of jazzy horizontals add vitality.
H. 3 3/4 in. x w. 22 1/4 in. (9.5 cm x 56.5 cm). S.J. & G.W. Lurie Collection.

Fig. 115. 1998. The whimsical side of Higashida. Three rigid wheels support, but cannot move, a three-sided vase with circular (shown here), square, and triangular decorations (not shown). Meaningless projections and squiggles are to be found on all surfaces. The collar is broken in two places. Doused with an Oribe glaze, it humorously plays with a host of ideas, including ambiguity, imperfection, self-contradiction, utility and the quality of workmanship.
H. 14 1/4 in. (36.2 cm). S.J. & G.W. Lurie Collection.

Fig. 116. 2003. A box to end all boxes: Higashida's magical, untamed, uninhabited craggy hills and forest—a natural paradise. Unfortunately, the complexity of this piece makes it virtually impossible for a photograph to do it justice.
H. 8 1/2 in. x w. 11 in. x d. 7 1/2 in. (21.5 cm x 27.9 cm x 19 cm). S.J. & G.W. Lurie Collection.

Fig. 117. 2003. This flower vase gives us a blue-white waterfall amidst rough rocks and deep mountain greenery. Each facet reveals an unexpected vista. The rocks sparkle like rough-cut jewels or glisten like morning dew on rocks in the wild. These are three views of one piece.

Fig. 117A, 117B. Two additional views of Fig. 117.
H. 12 in. (30.5 cm). S.J. & G.W. Lurie Collection.

Suzuki Goro
(b. 1941)
Suzuki Goro is the most unrestrained of today's Oribe artists. Suzuki seems to grandly distort everything he touches. His wild imagination can also be seen in his tirelessly painted decorations of comic strip cats, birds, dogs, doodles, naked women. He is known for his tea pots with crazy handles and spouts, unusual stacked boxes and weird chairs of all sizes. Most of his work is done in the usual Oribe colors of green and orange, typically with elaborate, good-natured, light-hearted detailing. The overall message conveyed by his work is that life and tradition are good and joyous, but not to be taken too seriously.

Figs. 118, 119. c. 2000. Suzuki's precariously balanced drinking cups have outlandish handles and random nutty embellishments. Surprisingly, they are, nevertheless, functional, although they look kooky, Oribe kooky. Both cups are seen together in one photograph. The large handle close-up of Fig. 119 is shown in full on p. 159. Fig. 118 is shown in another view on p. 159.

Fig. 118. H. 5 in. (12.7 cm). S.J. & G.W. Lurie Collection.
Fig. 119. H. 5.5 in. (14 cm). S.J. & G.W. Lurie Collection.

Fig. 120. 2001. The wacky back of this demented chair includes a distorted, broken orange plate. The seat is sagging. A normal chair epitomizes practical comfort but Suzuki, totally and humorously, undermines this expectation.

H. 41 in. (104 cm). Private collection, NY.

Fig. 121. 2002. Multi-layered boxes traditionally were not made from ceramics; they were made of wood and lacquer. However, Suzuki here gives us a three-layered ceramic box, festooned with freakishly unrelated jocular decorations. The cat has no idea why he is sitting beneath two light bulbs, one on and one off, nor do we.

H. 13 in. (33 cm). Private collection, NY.

Fig. 122. 1996. Rather than depicting a useful teapot, Suzuki gives us one with a massive, heavy handle and an enormous belly sitting atop a relatively narrow, high foot. Its crooked spout is so eccentrically twisted as to make it likely to pour onto the teapot itself, rather than into a teacup. Its handmade quality is stressed by the deep finger imprints that border much of the spout and handle. The swirling design on its body energizes this oversized, humorously ungainly proportioned teapot. It is illustrated against a background of a detail of Fig. 123.

H. 15.7 in. x w. 7.8 in. (40 cm x 20 cm) Private collection.

Fig. 123. c. 2000. It is not expected that a plate will be more than 12 inches in diameter, but Suzuki's plate is fit only for a giant of mythology, being 43 inches in diameter. This huge plate was deliberately broken, its pieces fired separately and then joined together, an homage to an historical practice of putting together precious old pottery shards to make a new piece. The illustrations—sexy, whimsical and vibrant—give a wishful vision of a potter's life. Prominently printed are the words "will you kiss" and "I love pot(s)." Does this mean pottery, marijuana, or both? The encroaching Oribe green and the rays of the electrical lightbulb, indicate nighttime. The potter is still working at his wheel. Within his square-shaped studio, a naked woman carries a heavy load of pots; another is expectantly lying on her back.

D. 43 in. (109.2 cm). Private collection, NY.

Takauchi Shugo
(b. 1937)

A visit to Mashiko inspired Takauchi to become a potter. Mashiko was, of course, the home base for Hamada Shoji, one of the founders of the Folk Art Movement in Japan. Not only was Takauchi inspired, but he moved to Mashiko, set up his kiln there, and continues to produce his work from that location. However, the only apparent influence on his work by the Folk Art Movement has been his preference for making ceramics for everyday use, including plates, platters, covered bowls, vases and water buckets. His spirit is not that of an anonymous folk potter, using a local style over and over again. He is a creative artist in both form and decoration, within the limitations imposed by the need to make functional pieces.

Fig. 124. c. 1980; **Fig. 125.** c. 2000. Takauchi, a prolific artist, has the ability to energize everyday ware, like the Oribe green glazed water bucket with boldly faceted areas adjacent to swirling, perhaps Jomon-inspired, patterns. Takauchi's large plate has a dark ghostly square set within a smooth circle, which is itself within a heavily-textured, irregularly-edged square. It does so much more than anyone would expect an apparently simple square platter to do.

W. 13 1/4 in. (33.7 cm). H. 15 in. (38.1 cm). S.J. & G.W. Lurie Collection.

FIG. 114. HIGASHIDA SHIGEMASA

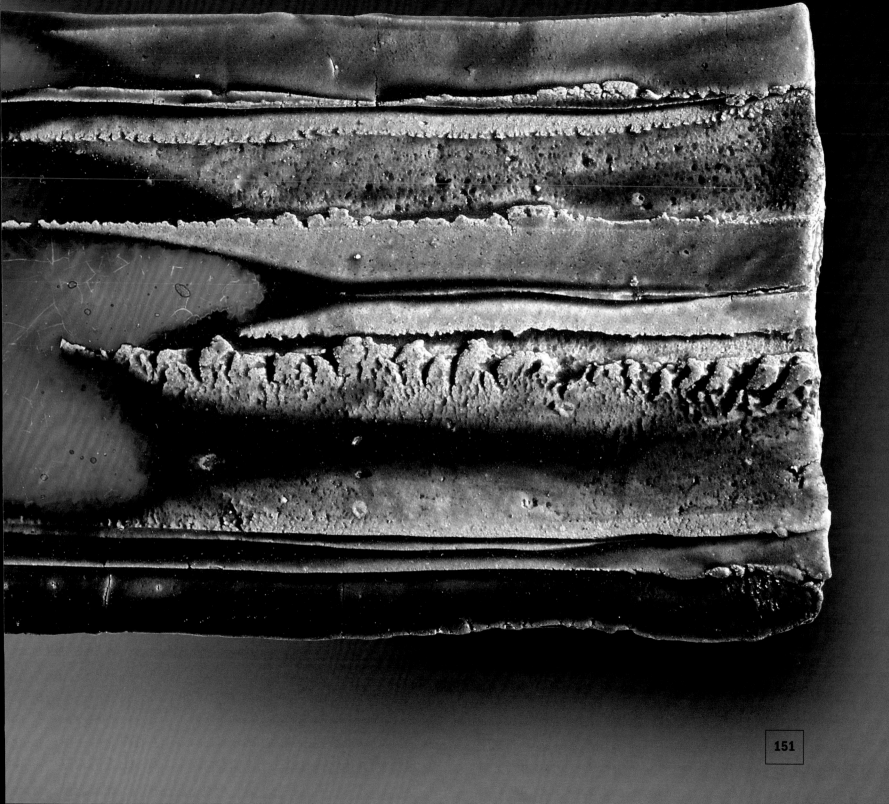

FIG. 115. HIGASHIDA SHIGEMASA

FIG. 116. HIGASHIDA SHIGEMASA.

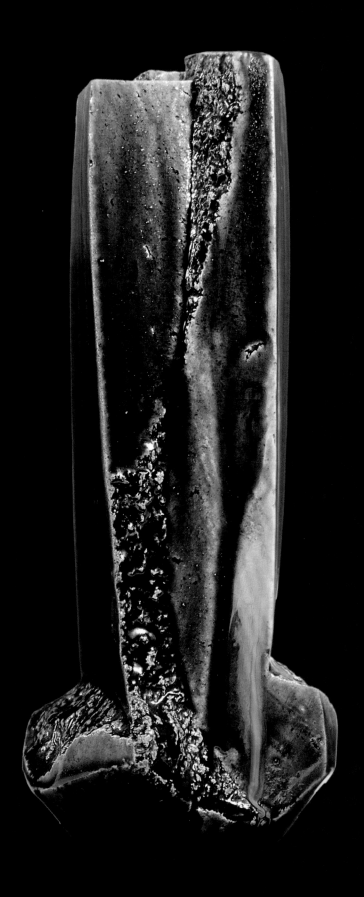
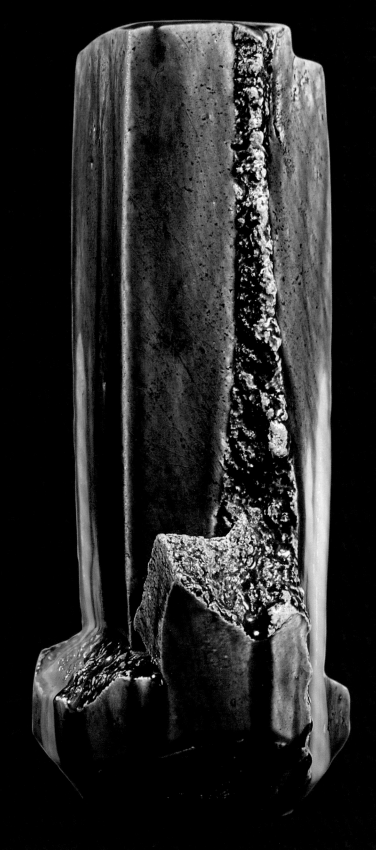

FIGS. 117A, 117B.
HIGASHIDA SHIGEMASA

FIG. 117. HIGASHIDA SHIGEMASA

FIGS. 118, 119. SUZUKI GORO

FIG. 120. SUZUKI GORO.

FIG. 121. SUZUKI GORO

FIG. 118. SUZUKI GORO
FIG. 119. SUZUKI GORO

159

FIG. 122. SUZUKI GORO

FIG. 123. SUZUKI GORO

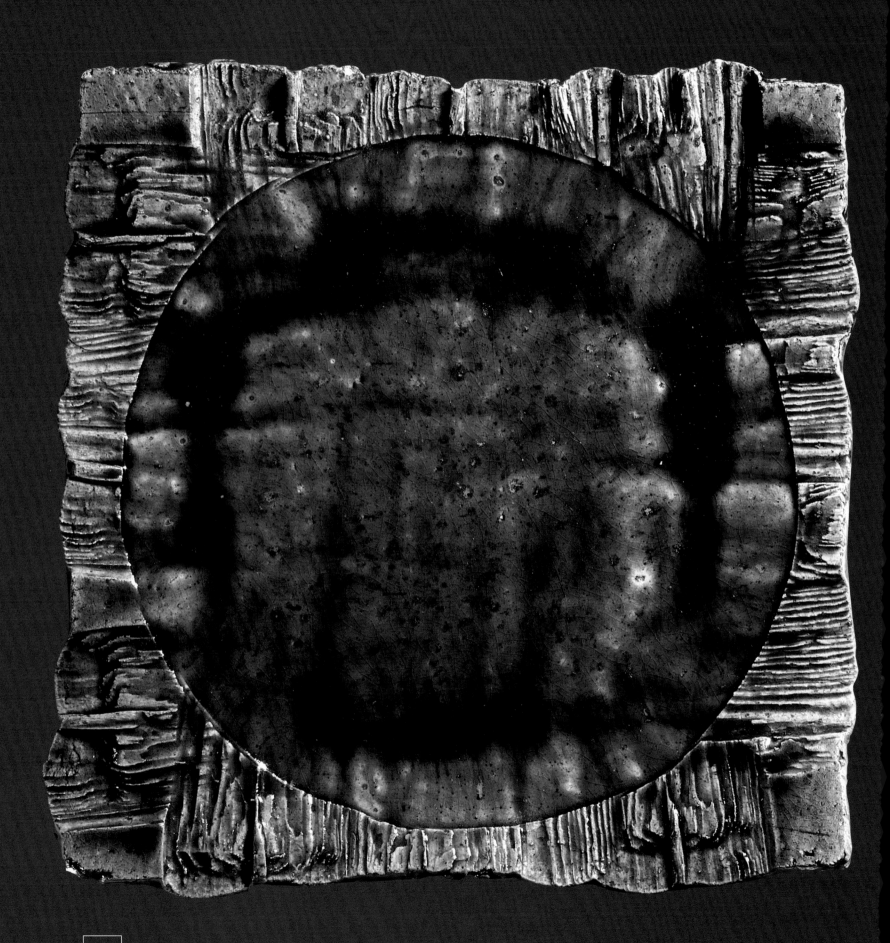

FIG. 124. TAKAUCHI SHUGO

FIG. 125. TAKAUCHI SHUGO

Gifu Region

FIGS. 126, 127. MOMOYAMA PERIOD

Gifu prefecture, or province, apart from its numerous hot springs and castles, is another historic pottery-making area that today produces a wide range of work. Interest now centers around the superb new Museum of Modern Ceramic Art, Gifu. Opened in late 2002, and designed by Isozaki Arata, it is one of the finest, if not the finest ceramic museum anywhere. Its mission is to collect and display modern and contemporary ceramic works from Japan and the rest of the world, to add "excitement and joy" (as stated in a museum brochure) to the lives of visitors. The entire feeling of the museum is in accordance with that wise purpose. The museum is about a 45 minute car ride from the city of Nagoya and about 1 1/2 hours from Osaka.

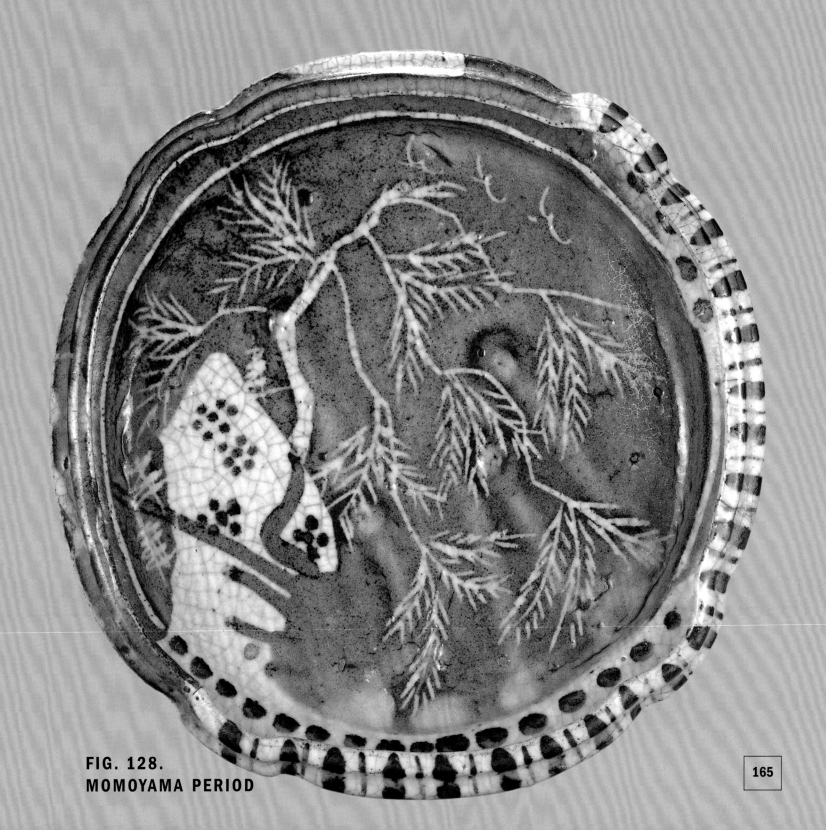

**FIG. 128.
MOMOYAMA PERIOD**

Gifu Region

Fig. 126. Momoyama Period (1568–1603). This solidly structured water jar, in Mino Iga style, was made in an area then called Mino, present-day Gifu. Unlike the usual natural glazed Iga water jars, this jar is covered by an applied, clear glaze. The two flowing brown streaks from added iron pigments, simulating Iga wood ash glaze, are signature elements of this style and serve to energize the body.

H. 7 in. x diam. 7 1/2 in. (17.8 cm x 19 cm). S.J. & G.W. Lurie Collection.

Fig. 127. Momoyama Period (1568–1603).Yellow Seto. This shallow bowl with a flower design, takes us into a realm of sweet innocence, of seemingly artless drawing, and shy hints of color—modest, lovable qualities, now, sadly, out of fashion.

H. 2 3/8 in. x diam. 11 3/8 in. (6 cm x 28.7 cm). Tokyo National Museum.

Fig. 128. Momoyama Period (1568–1603). Shino Ware. Its rim obeys no system, no regularity and no rule, except to please and surprise the eye and to avoid the sin of boredom. The tree branches and leaves dance the night away.

H. 3 1/2 in. x diam. 10 1/2 in. (8.9 cm x 26.6 cm). Suntory Museum of Art.

Arakawa Toyozo
(1894–1985)

In 1930, Arakawa discovered and excavated Momoyama kilns in the Gifu area where he found Shino shards, pottery fragments. This was a revelation at the time as Shino ware was formerly thought to have been made in a different location: Seto. More importantly, Arakawa's discovery fired the interest of other potter-excavators to discover other Momoyama kilns, to collect and study shards, and to produce work grounded on these ancient models. The resultant Momoyama revival was a broad enthusiastic increase in the appreciation of Momoyama tea ceremony ceramics. The Arakawa Toyozo Museum is located on the site of his discovery.

Fig. 129. *Grey Shino Dish with Mountain Design and Four Feet*, 1943. This sublime work was made in the middle of the horrors of the Second World War. It is notable for its tranquility and serenity. An abstract, possibly transparent, mountain is drawn by minimal double-curved lines. It is surmounted by three equally abbreviated pine trees which have a dancing, vibrant character. Shadowy blue clouds

hover above and, remarkably, a blue mist passes through the mountain. Two more fully realized, more stable, deciduous trees anchor the foot of the mountain.

H. 1 1/2 in. x w. 9 1/4 in. (3.8 cm x 23.5 cm). Toyozo Museum.

Fig. 130. *Himeji Castle*, 1972. An unequally proportioned vase, dressed in green-yellow armor, or suggesting a military fortification as indicated by its title. The middle row of rivet heads forms a low waist that helps the bottom balance the larger top half.

H. 10 1/2 in. (26.6 cm). Kiyoshikojin Seicho-ji Temple.

Fig. 131. *Yellow Seto Flower Vase*, 1953. This work embodies Arakawa's respect for a famous split bamboo flower vase and for the Momoyama aesthetic, which embraced kiln accidents—even to the extent of accepting an enormous crack that virtually splits the pot in half.

H. 10 1/2 in. (26.6 cm). Toyozo Museum.

Wakao Toshisada
(b. 1933)

Wakao was born into a family of potters in Tajimi City, where he still lives and works. At the end of World War II, his family was so poor that in 1948 Wakao left school and went to work in his father's kiln, which made functional vessels. After working all day with his father, he would return at night to make pottery that expressed his artistic preferences. He gradually developed a novel, painstaking technique for making a unique form of Shino ware, a process which requires very long firing in his kiln. He has written that skill comes in a decade, but pottery takes a lifetime and a half. Wakao, inherently modest, is eager to give credit for anything he has accomplished to forces outside of himself, like nature, clay, fire. He regards a ceramic surface to be like a canvass on which he paints. His hobbies are painting, photography, and collecting ancient Chinese shards, which also serve to sharpen his pictorial sensitivity.

Fig. 132. *Milky Way*. A view from below water level looking upwards through schematic ocean waves to a silvery half-moon and glittering gold and silver twinkling stars. Both *Milky Way* and *Melting Snow* are bathed in an otherworldly mystical ambiance, and both are poetic evocations which encourage one's imagination to freely roam.

L. 25 1/2 in. x w. 11 1/4 in. (64.7 cm x 28.5 cm). S.J. & G.W. Lurie Collection.

Fig. 133. *Melting Snow*, 2002. The moon is not directly in evidence, but there seems little doubt that the trees, sparkling with silver and golden highlights, reflect moonlight in this nighttime scene. The three whitish areas of snow are surrounded by dark gray areas of earth where the snow has already thawed. This work has a magical quality; the composition is masterful; the vertical trees are in unsteady tension with the three large, almost full-length horizontal sections.

L. 25 in. x w. 10 $1/2$ in. (63.5 cm x 26.6 cm). S.J. & G.W. Lurie Collection.

Figs. 134, 135. *Shino Boxes with Design*, 1992. Wakao's splendid boxes, infused with the spirit of romance, fit for holding treasured love letters, leave one struck by their sheer beauty. The subject matter is traditional; the artistry is exceptional. One hesitates to disrupt the complete composition, which extends from the lid down the sides, by opening, and actually using, this box.

H. 4 in. x l. 7 $1/2$ in. x d. 4 in. (10 cm x 19 cm x 10 cm). Private Collection.

Kato Sho
(1927–2001)

Kato Sho was a member of a family with a long pottery-making history. He spent his career at his family's Seto kiln, where he displayed his skill in a variety of styles, and managed to excel amidst the crowded group of Seto potters.

Fig. 136. 1983. This vase exudes an unassuming integrity. Its gritty clay has not been refined. There is a casual unconcern with the patternless distribution of green, blue-black and black colors. The faceting on the body, made by pushing wet clay upwards, contrasts with the plain long cylindrical neck. The curved ears lend weight to the neck and lock in an equilibrium with the body. A solid, satisfying work that is far from being as simple as it may first appear.

H. 7 $1/4$ in. (18.4 cm). S.J. & G.W. Lurie Collection.

Koie Ryoji
(b. 1938)

Koie Ryoji takes pride in both his extreme versatility as a ceramic artist and his hard-driving life style. In fact, they are inseparable. Koie himself is not shy about celebrating his working method: to drink a lot and to work a lot; believing that each beneficially fuels the other. His zest for life includes a love of music and piano playing. As a ceramist, his exuberance is expressed in the wide range of his work, from figurative and abstract sculpture, *avant garde* mixed-media installations, to functional pottery.

Fig. 137. *Return to Earth*, 1990. Using his own face as the subject, the artist, buried up to his head, literally shows the end of his own life. Before his face completely disintegrates, his expression is resigned, peaceful—a philosophical acceptance of the inevitable. At the end point, little remains of his face, which has turned into a pile of earth. His face, as well as his unseen body, have been returned to a primal condition ready to be reconstituted in another form.

H. 7$1/3$ in. x diam. 17 in. (18.7 cm x 43.2 cm). Private collection.

Nakashima Harumi
(b. 1950)

Nakashima Harumi was born in a farm area. His experience with the natural growing processes of plants, trees and vegetables made a deep impression, and became a major influence on his work as a ceramist. He studied with two important sculptural artists: Hayashi Yasuo and Kumakura Junkichi. Nakashima's career has combined his early fascination with plant growth with the challenging sculptural ideas from his two master teachers, leading Nakashima to make his unique biomorphic sculptures.

The basic component of his sculpture is the sphere covered with dots, both in a variety of sizes. The spheres and dots expand and contract. There are sinuous cylindrical connections among the spheres. Sometimes, the cylinders turn into a waving ribbon or collar form uniting the spheres. These sculptures are best viewed in the round, a full 360 degree circuit. The reward is a fascinating parade of delightful interrelated shapes. Looking at each piece as a whole, they may resemble something organic and growing. When two or more pieces are together, they seem to interact. Nakashima's works are open to a multiplicity of interpretations, but they always entrance the eye and are restlessly dynamic. They are alive.

Figs. 138, 139. *Struggling Forms* (2 pieces) 1997. **Fig. 140.** *Work,* 2004. One immediately senses the great delight of Nakashima's work. He achieves something rare and treasurable, in sculpture or art of any kind: his work makes you feel good, happy and giddy with pleasure. The pleasure, however, is not entirely innocent. It can be heavy with sensuality. Walking full circle around his organic forms provides changing delights, bouncy, active, often erotic, exuding sexual pheromones, almost inviting caressing.

Fig. 138. H. 30 $1/2$ in. x w. 19 $1/2$ in. (77.5 x 49.5 cm). S.J. & G.W. Lurie Collection;

Fig. 139. H. 29 $3/4$ in. x w. 19 $3/4$ in. (74.3 cm x 50 cm). S.J. & G.W. Lurie Collection;

Fig. 140. H. 9 $3/4$ in. x w. 22 $1/2$ in. (24.7 cm x 57 cm). Private collection.

Kato Kiyoyuki
(b. 1931)

Kato Kiyoyuki was born in Seto and still lives and works there. Until he reached his early twenties, he was primarily interested in painting. When he was in his early 30s, he already began winning prizes in important ceramic exhibitions. He has continued to exhibit widely in Japan.

Fig. 141. *Work.* This clean, rectangular form, coldly separated into light and dark areas, has all the icy resonance of a contemporary minimalist exercise. Then one happily sees the unmistakable evidence of human presence, like a footprint on a deserted beach. Someone has run a finger deeply across the wet clay surface and has also made a primitive flower-like image. It can be analyzed as containing allusions to both contemporary and primitive art, or to opposing qualities in general, such as expressions of freedom and restraint, or sophistication and naivete, night and day, pre-human darkness and the rise of primitive civilization. Composed of just a few elements, it stimulates the widest imaginative excursions.

H. 17.7 in. (45 cm). Aichi Prefectural Ceramic Museum.

Fig. 142. *Work 72-F,* 1972. Kato Kiyoyuki has had a long-standing fascination with the decay and abandonment of structures. Shaped a bit like a decaying Pre-Columbian temple, its outer walls have mostly been lost, exposing the cramped structure under the surface. This may have been a habitation long ago, but it has been left to disintegrate over time, leaving a grim memorial. These ruins may be explained as the result of violence, of war, or, since there is no evidence of smoke, charring or fire, perhaps it is the result of an ecological disaster, such as an abused environment that could no longer support the population. It reminds one of the abandonment in the 14th century by the Anasazi Indians of their settlements in the American southwest, for reasons still unknown.

H. 24 in. x w. 18 1/2 in. x 12 1/4 in. (61 cm x 46.9 cm x 31.1 cm). Aichi Prefectural Ceramic Museum.

Kato Tsubusa
(b. 1962)

Kato Tsubusa was born in Tajimi City. Starting from age 21, he has worked exclusively with white porcelain clay. Although this clay is harder to handle, he prefers it because it is snow white. Porcelain is invariably associated with the Chinese porcelain aesthetic: refined, flawlessly balanced in form, delicate, serene, elegant, in short, perfect. The work of Kato Tsubusa, with subtle pale blue celadon glazing, is no less beautiful than traditional porcelain, but in much different ways. Kato's porcelain sculpture manifests motion, not tranquility; "flawed" adventurous forms, not examples of impeccably executed familiar forms; dramatically sweeping, not refined stillness. Some of his pieces, such as his tea bowls, can easily be put to actual use. Others can be used, in theory, only if one is willing to risk the razor-sharp edges and daunting fragility of his "vases" and "bowls."

Figs. 143, 144. *Bowls with Square Sides,* 2003, 2005, respectively. The two bowls together provide visible evidence of Kato's creative development. The less radical bowl (fig. 143) is already far down the road of confronting the aesthetic standards of traditional celadon bowls. The sides of this bowl are neither straight nor round, they are warped, sharply edged, incompletely glazed with random celadon pools, seemingly unplanned grooved sides, and asymmetric. These heresies are carried even further in Kato's second bowl, made two years later (fig. 144). Now the sides are of different heights, and lean so perilously they provoke fear of collapse. One side is badly split and its corners are even more violently jagged. The evolving forms clearly are intended to test the limits of how far departures can be made from accepted traditional standards and still retain the essential beauty which is the basic reason one is interested in looking at this work. We are anxious to see where Kato takes us next.

Fig. 143. H. 5 in. x w. 15 3/4 in. x l. 16 1/2 in. (12.7 cm x 40 cm x 42 cm). S.J. & G.W. Lurie Collection.

Fig. 144. H. 8 in. x w. 15 in. x l. 15 in. (20.3 cm x 38 cm x 38 cm). S.J. & G.W. Lurie Collection.

Fig. 145. *Freeze Flame*, c. 2002. The celadon glaze has pooled in the center forming a lake, unfortunately barely visible on this photograph, that could only exist in paradise. It calls up a wealth of associations. Is it surrounded by white, snow-covered jagged mountains, or are they cresting arctic waves, or teased abstract soaring fingers of energy, of ice or frozen flames? Part of the facination of this piece is that all of these interpretations are persuasive.

H. 6 1/2 in. x d. 8 3/4 in. x l. 11 3/4 in. (16.5 cm x 22.2 cm x 29.8 cm). S.J. & G.W. Lurie Collection.

Fig. 146. *Object*, 2005. Kato accepts the challenge of working with clay in its most difficult, fragile form: long strips of stretched clay supported at only one end. At the apex of the tall triangular body, one long strip reaches skyward and another, almost a continuation, points to the ground, like the outstretched arms of a ballerina. A better comparison is to the art of calligraphy. The long, vibrant strips of clay resemble calligraphic strokes. Energy. Pure energy in clay embodying dashing calligraphy. The glaze, continuing the action, flows downwards, finally collecting in pools.

H. 36 in. x w. 24 in. (91.4 cm x 60.9 cm). Private collection.

Fig. 147. *Flower Vase*, c. 2003. This is a masterpiece in a small package. Its tiny fragile lip demands gentle care in handling, like a newborn. The flowing immaculate celadon has covered only a portion of the body, pooling to form a tiny extended foot. The contrast between the cool, smooth celadon and the dry unglazed white clay body adds a tactile quality. Each facet presents a subtly different profile. This work is a mixture of original rawness, evidence of process, ending in the sublime.

H. 7 in. x w. 4 1/2 in. (17.7 cm x 11.4 cm). S.J. & G.W. Lurie Collection.

Imura Toshimi
(b. 1961)

Imura Toshimi studied sculpture at Kanazawa University, and then went on to study ceramics at Tajimi Technical High School. He grew up in a potters' family, both his parents making traditional pottery. Although his work is far different, he demonstrates his deep respect for his parents and their work by displaying their work in a reception area of his home in Gifu.

Figs. 148, 149. *Growing.* **Figs. 150, 151.** 2004, *Hollow*, 1997. Almost all, if not all, abstract ceramic sculptors are concerned with the outer appearance, or form, of their work, but Imura is as interested in the interior of his pieces as much as the exterior. He refers to the outer surface as "skin," which necessarily reminds us that there must be body structures beneath the skin. Imura is keenly interested in the interaction between the outer and inner spaces, and he refers to a tense equilibrium between the skin of his works and their inner structures. His interior structures are usually not practical necessities, but, instead, are driven by aesthetic considerations. To further complicate matters, the walls of the inner structures can be seen as becoming skins while creating an assemblage of new interlocking spaces. In works where the inner structures are as prominently visible as the skins, the impact of the outer skins is enhanced by being burnished to a high metallic sheen.

A special strength is that his work gains in fascination when seen from different viewpoints. Figs. 148 and 149 are photographs of one piece from two different angles, almost arbitrarily chosen from a larger number which are equally interesting. Similarly, fig. 151 is a detail of fig. 150 and it shows the strange beauty of the intricate inner structures, complemented by the unsurprisingly pleasant outer forms.

Figs. 148, 149. H. 14 in. x w. 16 in. x d. 13 in. (35 cm x 40 cm x 33 cm). Private collection.

Figs. 150, 151. H. 26 in. x w. 34 in. x d. 24 in. (65 cm x 87 cm x 60 cm). Private collection.

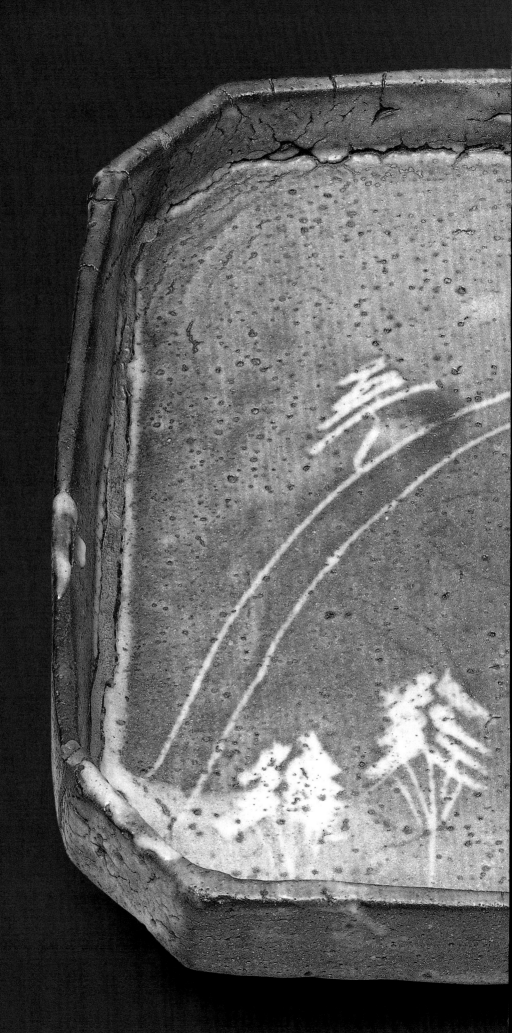

FIG. 129. ARAKAWA TOYOZO

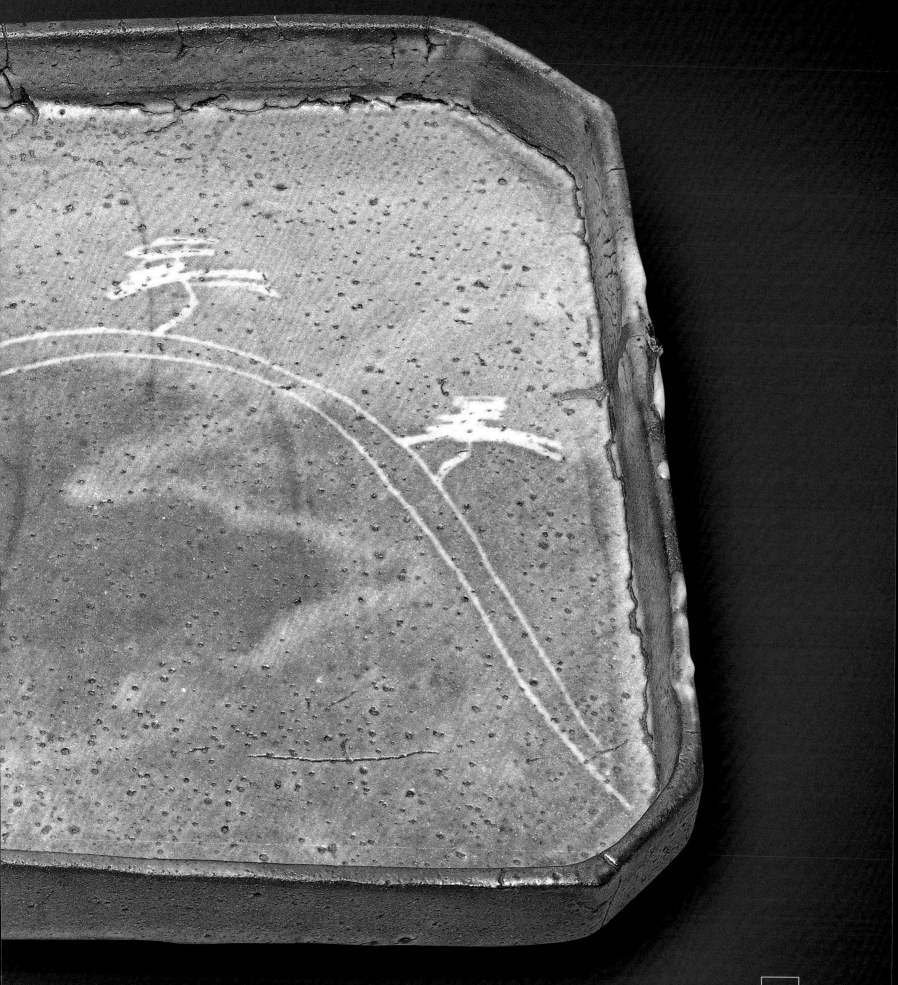

FIG. 130. ARAKAWA TOYOZO

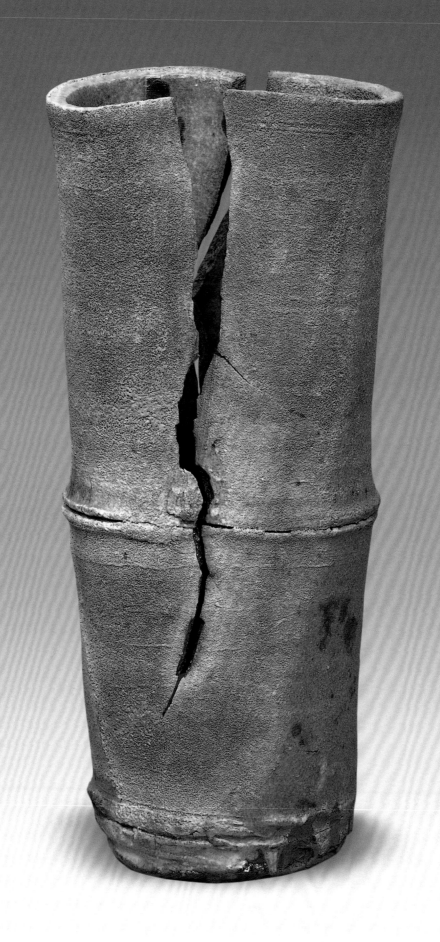

FIG. 131. ARAKAWA TOYOZO

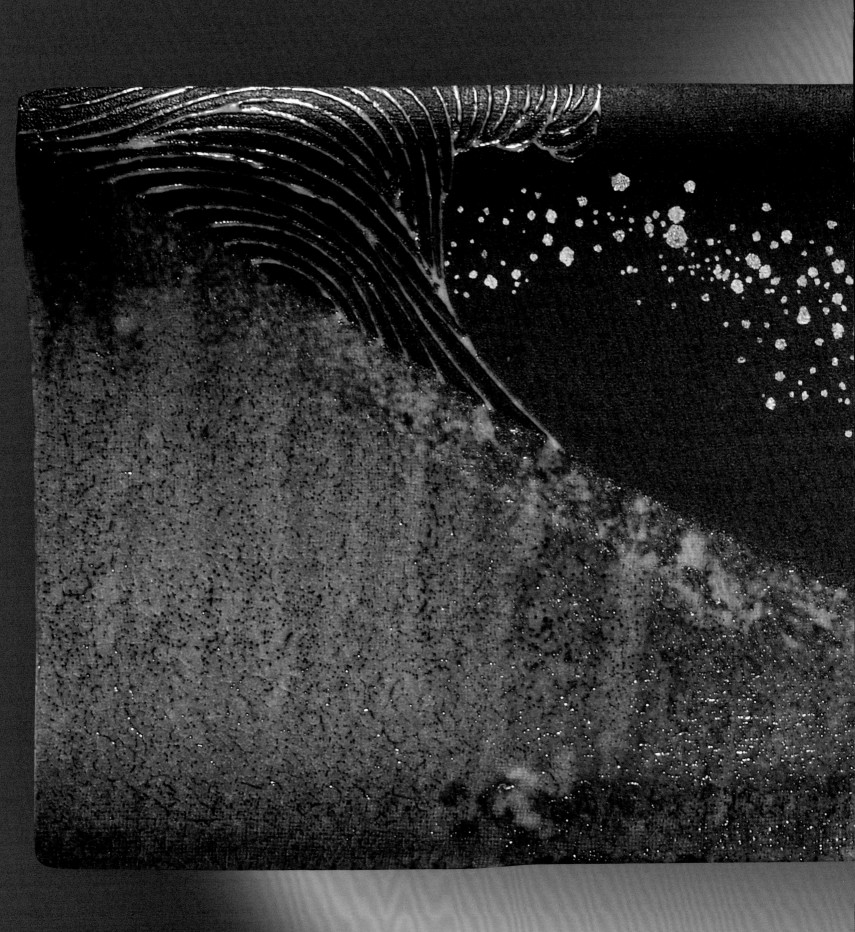

FIG. 132. WAKAO TOSHISADA

FIG. 133. WAKAO TOSHISADA

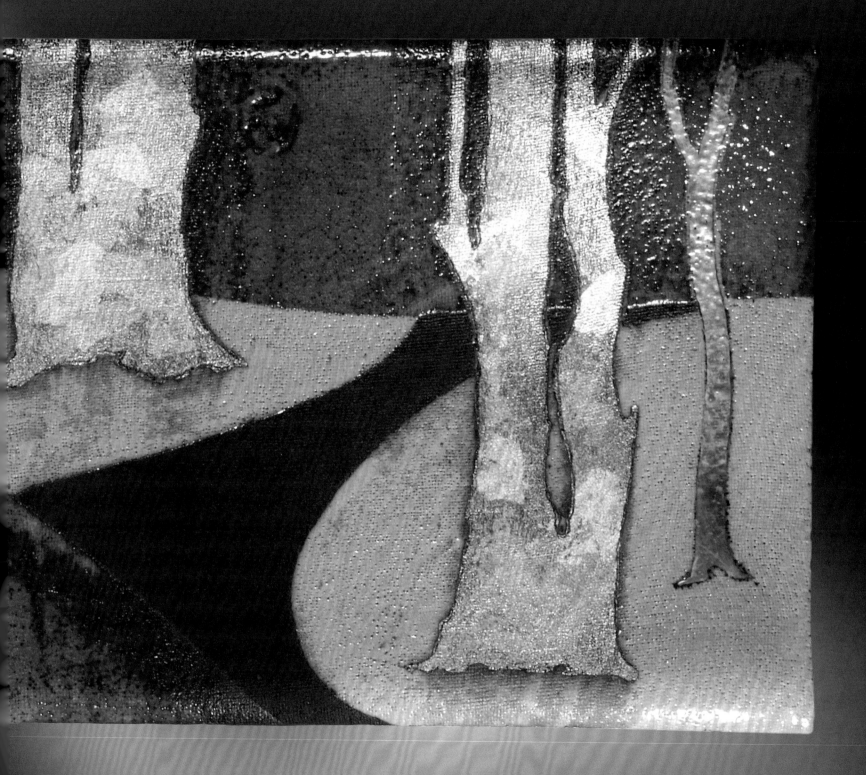

FIG. 134. WAKAO TOSHISADA

FIG. 135. WAKAO TOSHISADA

FIG. 136. KATO SHO

FIG. 137 KOIE RYOJI

FIG. 138. NAKASHIMA HARUMI

FIG. 139. NAKASHIMA HARUMI

FIG. 140. NAKASHIMA HARUMI

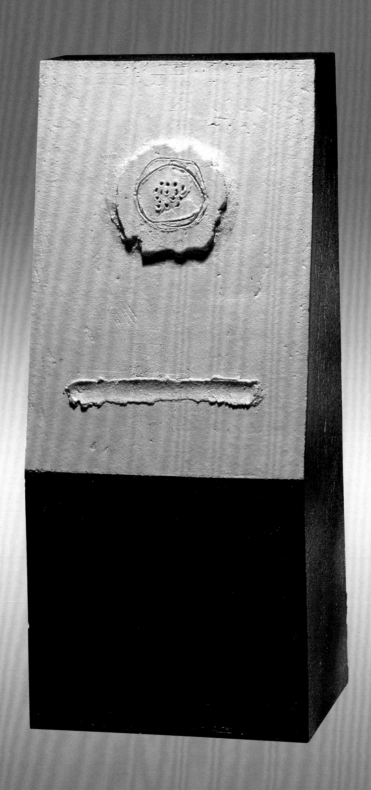

FIG. 141. KATO KIYOYUKI

FIG. 142. KATO KIYOYUKI

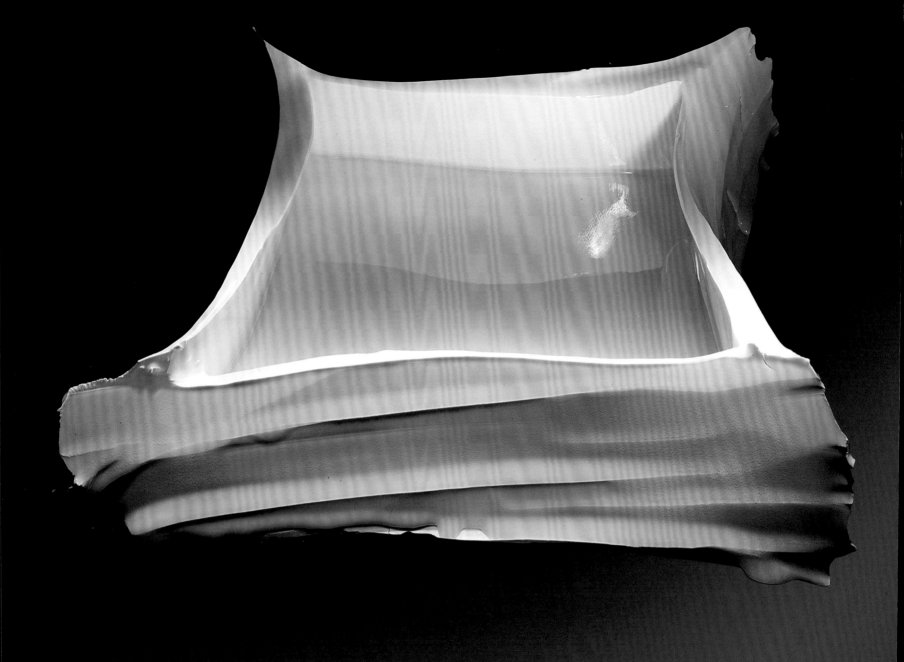

FIG. 143. KATO TSUBUSA

FIG. 144. KATO TSUBUSA

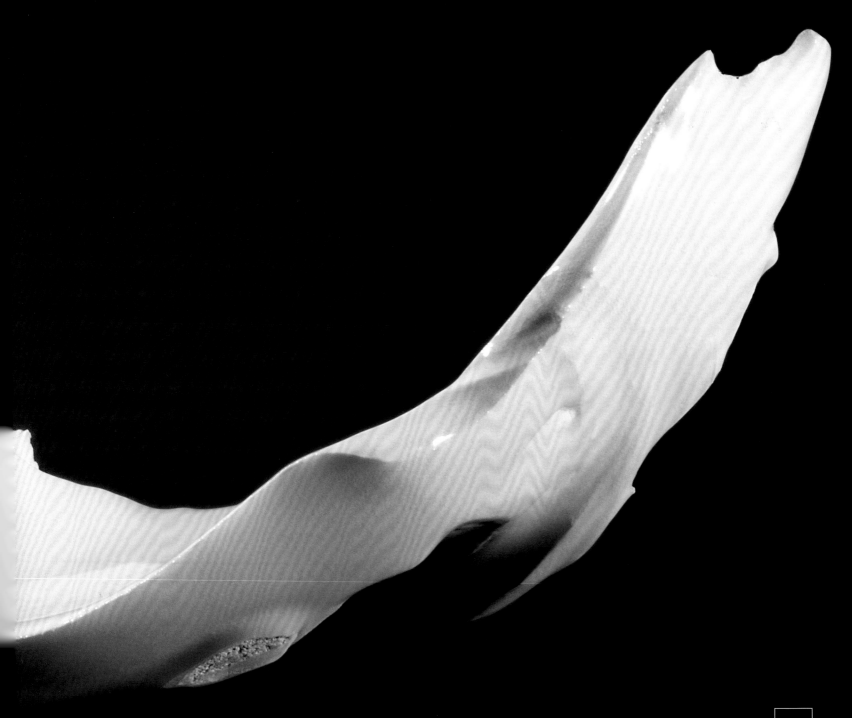

FIG. 145. KATO TSUBUSA

FIG. 146. KATO TSUBUSA

FIG. 147. KATO TSUBUSA

194

FIGS. 148, 149, 150.
IMURA TOSHIMI

FIG. 151. IMURA TOSHIMI

195

Tokyo Region

Tokyo did not begin its rise as a major world capital until the early 17th century. Although a late starter, it now is a leading cultural center, as well, of course, as the seat of government, commerce and finance.

Literally dozens of museums, public and private, can be found here. Some feature their own ceramic collections and regularly hold ceramic exhibitions. Universities offer courses in ceramics, both practical and theoretical. Some of the great department stores, such as Mitsukoshi, Takashimaya and Wako, continue their tradition of weekly ceramic selling exhibitions. Art galleries are scattered about the city, and many concentrate on showing Japanese ceramics, old and new. Professional ceramists maintain kilns on the outskirts of Tokyo. In short, ceramics play a significant role in the cultural life of Tokyo, a fact easily verified by observing the large crowds ceramic exhibitions draw, numbers beyond the imagination of Western art lovers.

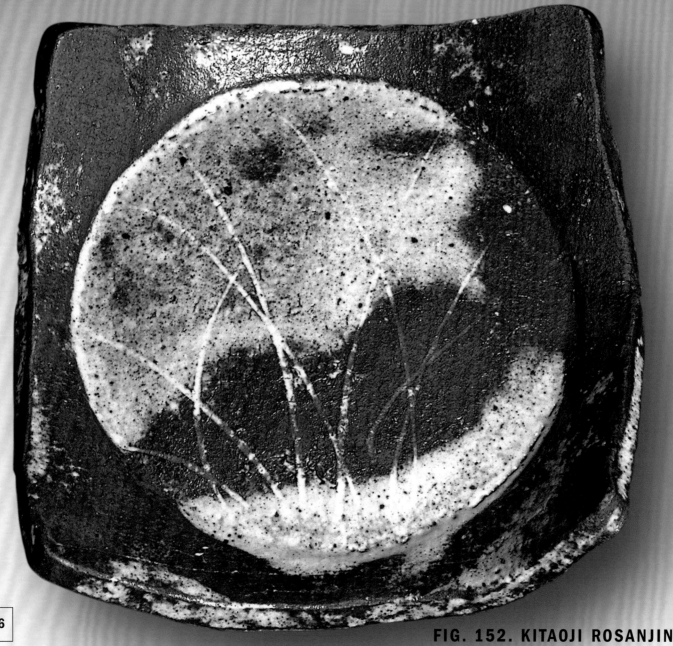

196

FIG. 152. KITAOJI ROSANJIN

FIGS. 153, 154. KITAOJI ROSANJIN

Kitaoji Rosanjin
(1883–1959)

Rosanjin was, perhaps, the most colorful Japanese potter of modern times. His friend and collector, Sidney Cardozo, has described Rosanjin using the following words: outspoken, cantankerous, tempestuous, infuriating, and a man whose boorishness had become almost legendary. Cardozo added that Rosanjin also was brilliant, eccentric, remarkable, kind and generous. His negative qualities would stand out in any Western society, but in Japan, where quiet, polite manners are the norm and confrontations avoided, Rosanjin's character was infinitely more unexpected.

Rosanjin's early years were spent in abject poverty and in the absence of both parents. He first attained success as a calligrapher, starting a career as a carver of wooden shop signs and seals. He then went on to become a collector and dealer in antiquities, a gourmet chef and, finally, a largely self-taught potter.

Rosanjin became interested in pottery, quite literally, through his belly. He was the owner of a fine restaurant in Tokyo but became dissatisfied with the dishes made by others, upon which his food was being served. He believed that "delicious food needs dishes with appropriate beauty, otherwise it complains of incompletion." At the age of 42 he began making his own pottery and later became a professional potter. Rosanjin is best known for the large number of ceramic styles that he worked in, which included his favorites, Oribe, Shino, Bizen, Iga, Shigaraki and Seto styles, as well as enameled porcelain. See fig. 47B for his Oribe style fig. 152 for his Shino style, and figs. 153-154 for his enamel work, both under Ogata's influence.

The esteem in which Rosanjin was held by some of his peers is shown in the following story. Sidney Cardozo relates that Kaneshige Toyo, at the height of his own success, came to Rosanjin's work shop and built for Rosanjin a climbing kiln for the firing of Bizen ware, in order to spare Rosanjin the time and difficulty of traveling to Bizen to do his firings.

Cardozo also relates another story which may strike one today as humorous, but which enraged Rosanjin. In May 1954, Rosanjin visited Picasso in Vallauris, France, a pottery center where Picasso was then working with clay. Rosanjin presented one of his works to Picasso, contained, as is customary, in a beautiful wood box. Picasso made it very clear that he loved the box, stroking its smooth surface, but showed no inclination to open the box to look at the pot. Predictably, Rosanjin exploded at Picasso, then elderly and covered with world honors as a secular deity, "Not the box, you simple child! What I made is inside the box."

Although Rosanjin had a deserved reputation as a lover of fine Japanese food, and of beer and other alcoholic drinks, he was also a prodigious worker making, according to Cardozo, an astounding number of pieces during his career. He was also a collector, but again, according to Cardozo, on a scale so stupendous as to invite the interest of a psychologist. He particularly liked and collected works by Ogata Kenzan.

Rosanjin detested the Folk Art Movement, which idealized the anonymous, traditional potter. Quite the opposite, he strove to express his individual, creative ability to make beautiful pottery. He recognized no worldly authorities and, on two occasions, refused to accept the designation of Living National Treasure.

Rosanjin also had a relationship with Isamu Noguchi, whom he mentored in clay work. We should also not forget that he gave financial aid to his then assistant, Arakawa, when Arakawa was doing excavations to find the source of Shino ware.

Fig. 152. *Shino Square Bowl*. 1957. Against a background of autumnal red, Rosanjin uses white Shino glaze to freely create a fantasy of grass and clouds within a full moon shape.
W. 8 3/4 in. (22.2 cm). Private collection.

Fig. 153. *Bowl with Overglaze Enamels of Camellias*, 1935–1984; **Fig. 154.** *Bowl With Cherry Blossoms & Maple Tree*, 1935–1944. These are two large deep bowls, not tea bowls. They depict late winter and early spring (camellias) and spring/autumn (cherry blossoms and maple leaves). They were designed by Rosanjin to reflect the pleasures of the seasons in connection with the food being served. The excitement of enjoying good food, served in fine ceramics, is perfectly realized.
H. 4 1/4 in. (10.8 cm). Setagaya Museum of Art.
H. 4 1/2 in. (11.4 cm). Setagaya Museum of Art.

Koike Shoko
(b. 1943)

Overthrowing stereotypes of delicate female sensibility, Koike Shoko has earned success in the male-dominated field of ceramic art in Japan. Her powerful forms, derived from shells, are bursting with energy and evoke a potent organic presence.

Fig. 155. *Work*, 1997. Gritty Shigaraki clay has been transformed into open, spiky shell-like claws, just emerging from the sea. Its claws are not harmlessly frozen; they are menacing. They will devour and destroy prey that its glowing interior has lured. It may also be interpreted as a womb-like opening, suggesting mother-earth fertility and receptivity.
H. 13 in. x w. 20 1/4 in. (33 cm x 51.4 cm). S.L. & G.W. Lurie Collection.

Fig. 156. *Shell*, 2004. An image of a mighty covered seashell with ridges seemingly swaying in motion, partly buried in the ocean bottom, housing an impressive lord of its domain. The ridges rhythmically dance around the entire circumference, proud of their beauty and strength.
H. 16 in. x w. 17 in. (40.6 cm x 43.2 cm). S.L. & G.W. Lurie Collection.

Matsuda Yuriko
(b. 1943)

Matsuda Yuriko has a singular and important role in contemporary Japanese ceramics. She injects a zest for outsized colorful and playful renditions of overly familiar subjects that are sometimes sexy, but are always bright and cheerful. Her signature works include body parts, often life-sized, decorated with a plethora of brash, vivid images, including flowers, Chinese characters, and numerous textile design references, and vegetables transformed into teapots and plates. Her easy, light, radiant format can, nevertheless, express her deeply involved cultural references.

Fig. 157. *Thunder Storm*, 1989. An extravagant assemblage of pop-inspired playful gold, purple and green lightening bolts, a rain cloud, stylized comically oversized snow and hail in entirely inappropriate colors. The colors are so outrageous that they become hilariously acceptable.

H. 13 in. (33 cm). Private collection.

Fig. 158. *Cherry Tree and Mt. Fuji*, 1998. Matsuda, who lives within sight of Mt. Fuji, takes Mt. Fuji and cherry blossoms, among the most celebrated subjects in Japanese art, and gives them her unique twist. Mt. Fuji is now fair game for her comic imagination. Six cherry blossom trees are not only tremendously oversized, but some also are growing so far beyond the mountainside that they appear to be poised to either fly off Mt. Fuji, or to fly away carrying Mt. Fuji with them. Mt. Fuji, a symbol of Japan, is appropriately wrapped in prestigious gold like traditional Japanese screen backgrounds. A nearby blue lake finds itself halfway up Mt. Fuji, which is topped by year-round pure white snow.

H. 20 1/4 in. x w. 17 7/8 in. (51.4 cm x 45.4cm). S.J. & G.W. Lurie Collection.

Fig. 159. *La Priere*, or *The Prayer*, 2000. An apparent duality is present. Although in a prayer position, very few viewers will consider this a religious subject—unless sex is their religion. With great humor, Matsuda provocatively shows a splendid tattooed derriere, a tiny thong her only concession to modesty. The elaborate foot tattoos are paradisiacal to a foot fetishist, and humorous to others who are surprised by the decorative abundance lavished on soles of the feet, which are so rarely seen. However, it should be remembered that Japan has a long-standing body tattooing culture. An ultimate purpose of prayer is for long life and Matsuda has painted the character for longevity on the soles of both feet. This may have been inspired by the traditional practice of Indian and Pakistani women who use foot tattoos as a beauty enhancement.

H. 14 in. x w. 15 in. x d. 7 1/2 in (35.5 cm x 38.1 cm x 19 cm). S.J. & G.W. Lurie Collection.

Onodera Gen
(b. 1934)

Born in Hokaido, Japan's most northern island, Onodera Gen trained in art school and apprenticed with Rosanjin before establishing his own kiln. He fell in love with early Japanese ceramics, going back as far as Sue ware. Onodera collects ancient shards and believes that black ware offers endless possibilities that are well-suited to the subdued, understated approach that he favors. He is a meticulous craftsman, keeping detailed documentation of his firings.

Fig. 160. 1980. It is not difficult to recognize the faultless restrained qualities of Onodera Gen's basket. He makes us appreciate that expressive form need not be operatic to be effective; that artistry can encourage the viewer to look more closely, avoiding habitual superficiality. Only by the use of sharpened perceptions will one have the pleasure of discovering the subtle decorative parallel lines beneath its rim, the small variations in the width of its strap handle, the harmonious relationship between its oval shaped body, sides and handle. This is a work that calls to mind words like integrity, quiet beauty, self-effacement and inducing meditation. It effortlessly makes a big statement. By itself, it is austerely perfect; with a single flower, it is brought to a fuller life. This work was previously owned by Sidney Cardozo, a connoisseur of Japanese pottery, and like Onodera's piece, without pretension, but highly accomplished.

H. 8 3/4 in. x w. 10 1/4 in. x l. 13 in. (22.2 cm x 26 cm x 33 cm). S.J. & G.W. Lurie Collection.

Fig. 160A. Another view of Fig. 160.

Nakamura Kimpei
(b. 1935)

At the age of 20, Nakamura left the sculptural department of art school to study cooking, yes, cooking, and Rosanjin's ware. In 1969, Nakamura, already 34, made his first trip to the U.S.A., which he later described as a "shock," "...as if I had got in a time machine and traveled from the Edo Period to the twentieth century." Returning to Japan, he started a contemporary ceramics program at Tama Art University. He became an influential art professor, tirelessly preaching the gospel of international ceramic art.

Nakamura constructs piles of natural and artificial bits and pieces resembling junk and broken things. His work flirts with being good-looking trash, offering attractive whiffs of color and sculptural form. Work that is merely a revolting pile of garbage would repel us, but some of his work is beautiful in an off-beat way. Nakamura wants his work to hold our attention, to focus on the problems, inadequacies and vulgarities in Japanese society that they illustrate and that he wishes to reform. He is a social critic, a cultural critic, a man who despises kitsch in all its forms.

Fig. 161. *An Exploration of Japanese Taste, Sumptuousness and Untruth*, 1991. A mass of disjointed chunks of stuff, products of a wasteful society, tricked out with shoddy painting that fails to improve their appearance. The mindless destruction of our forests for reasons of unchecked greed is referenced by a tree limb painted an appropriate gold color. Messy, like Japan's anarchic urban sprawlscapes, but tingling with life. Although Nakamura is critical, his title asserts that people, unfortunately, actually like this trash.

H. 31 1/2 in. x w. 26 3/4 in. x d. 18 1/2 in. (80 cm x 67.9 cm x 46 cm). Aichi Prefectural Ceramic Museum.

Fig. 161A. A detail of Fig. 161.

FIG. 155. KOIKE SHOKO

FIG. 156. KOIKE SHOKO

FIG. 157. MATSUDA YURIKO

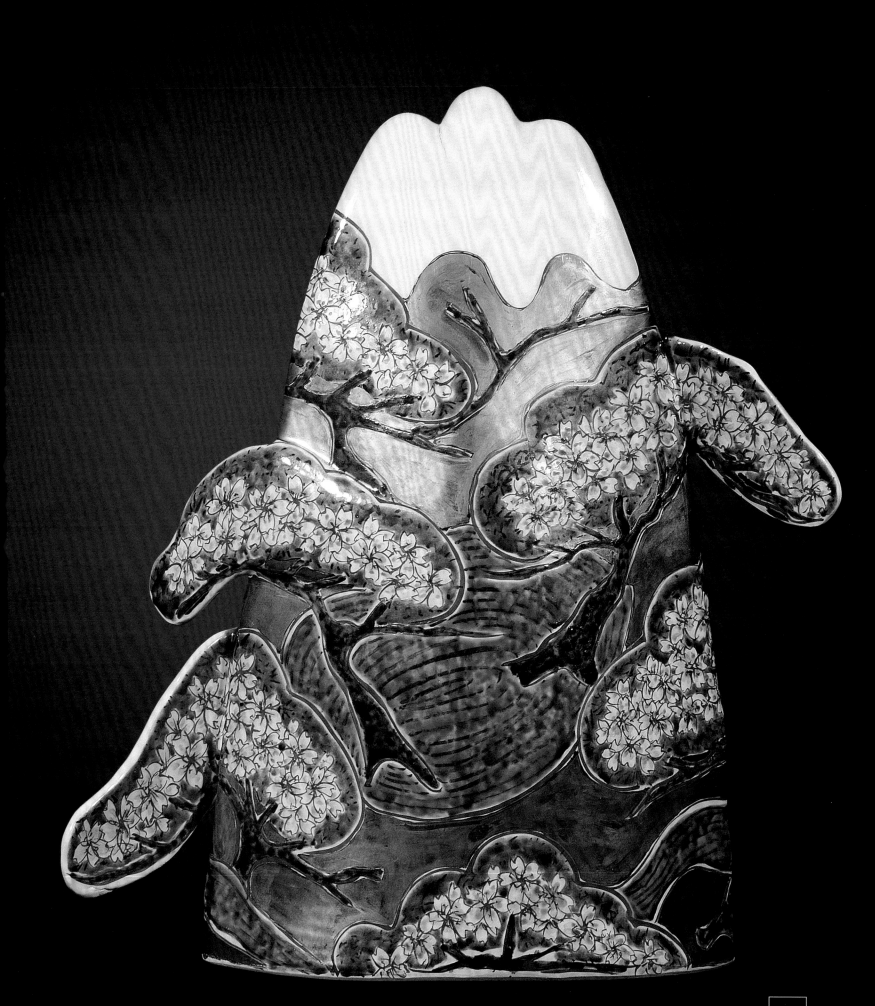

FIG. 158. MATSUDA YURIKO

FIG. 159. MATSUDA YURIKO

207

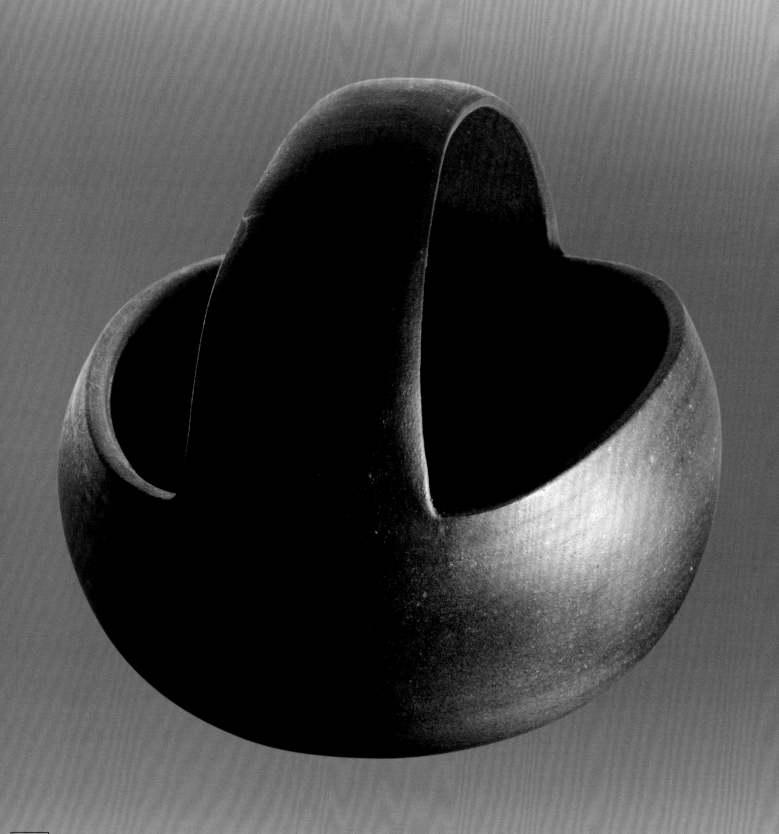

FIG. 160. ONODERA GEN

FIG. 160A. ONODERA GEN

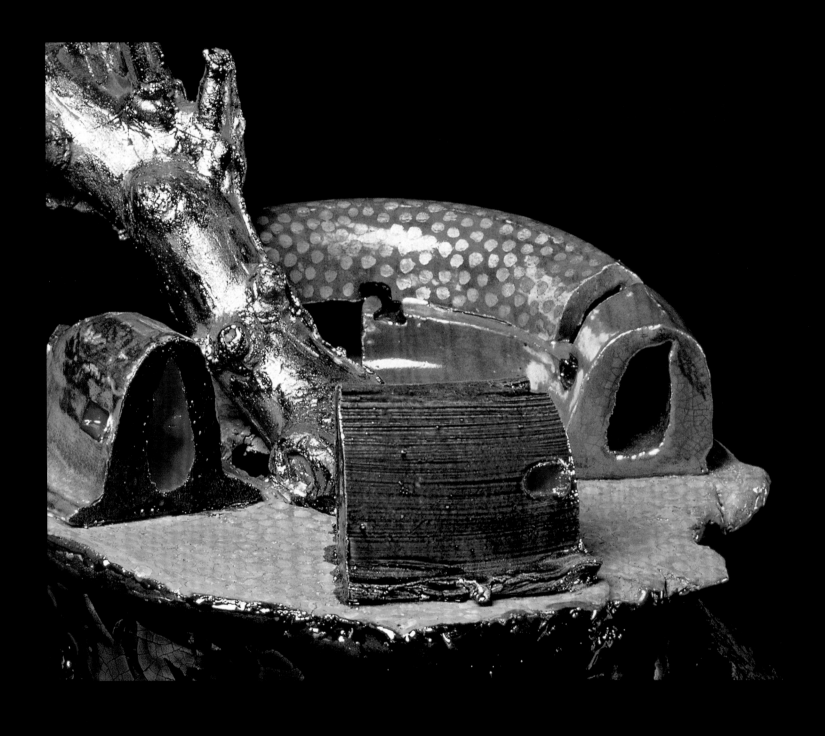

FIG. 161A. NAKAMURA KIMPEI

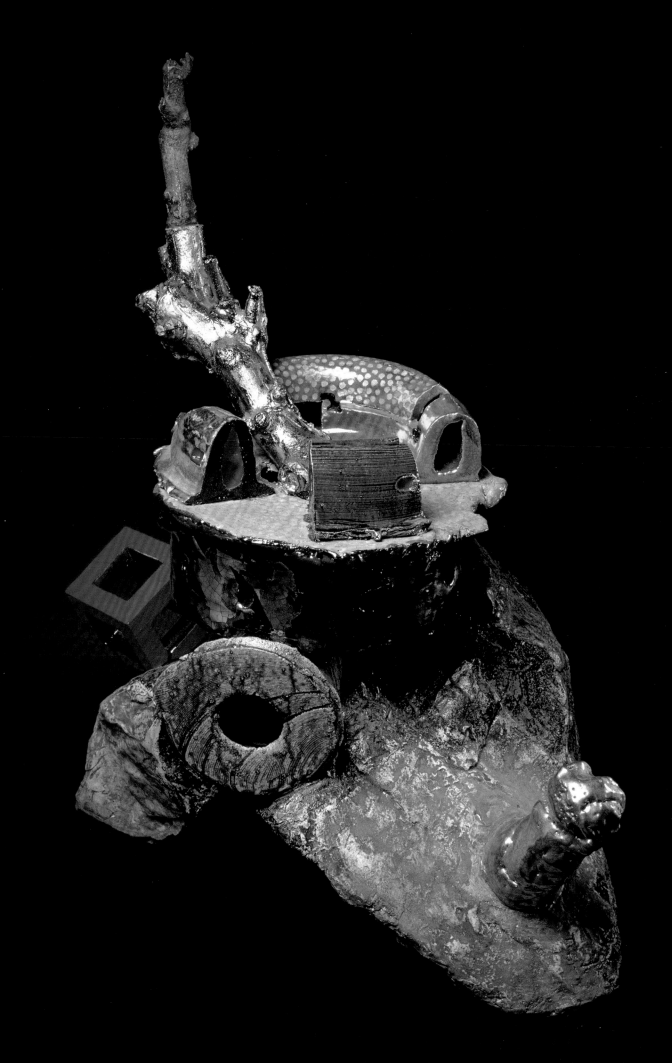

FIG. 161. NAKAMURA KIMPEI

Mashiko and Other Regions

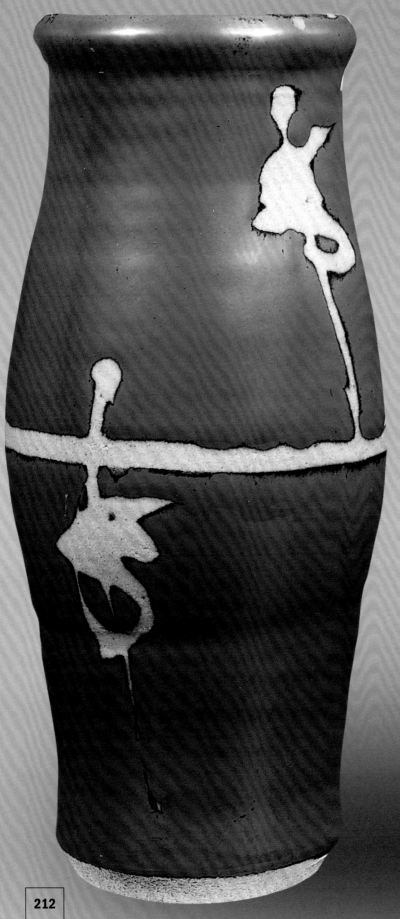

Mashiko is a city about three hours north of Tokyo by automobile. The city is indelibly associated with the Mingei, or Folk Art Movement, because Hamada Shoji, a movement founder, established his kiln in Mashiko. Today, many potters, not necessarily folk potters, have established their kilns either in Mashiko or on its outskirts. Hamada's kiln compound has been turned into a museum to which many potters and ceramic lovers make a pilgrimage.

FIG. 162. HAMADA SHOJI

Hamada Shoji

(1894–1978)

Hamada is certainly the best-known Japanese potter in the West, which he frequently visited. He had a close relationship and working partnership with the important British potter, Bernard Leach (1887–1979), with whom he set up a Japanese style kiln in St. Ives, in southwest England. Hamada toured the U.S. on many occasions, lecturing, giving workshops, and being a great ambassador for folk-based Japanese ceramics. His pottery style has proven to be easily accessible and popular.

Hamada is also closely associated with two other great names in Japanese ceramics. While a student in a Tokyo high school, he met Kawai Kanjiro, with whom he began a lifelong friendship, and he studied under Itaya Hazan.

Hamada adhered, partially, to the folk idea of the anonymous craftsman. He refused to carve his signature or impress his seal into the pots that he made. However, that did not prevent him from signing the wood boxes in which they were contained. In theory, Hamada did not want to appear to be an artist who intellectually or self-consciously created works of ceramic art. He liked to think that he himself did not produce his work, that it, somehow, was the product of a collective community effort, rather than by his unaided labor. Consistent with the folk craft ideal, he only made utilitarian pieces.

Fig. 162. c. 1950. Against a luscious persimmon background, balletic figures dance, or are they a kind of dynamic calligraphy? In either case, they are sketched with remarkable economy and eloquence. Hamada used a wax-resist painting technique to produce the figures or characters which encircle the vase. These are three views of one piece.

H. 11 1/4 in. x w. 5 1/8 in. (28.6 cm x 13 cm). S.J. & G.W. Lurie Collection.

Fig. 163. 1960s. Hamada uses this six-sided mold-impressed vase as a pallette for a gorgeous display of color, inspired by the lesser-known Okinawa folk pottery tradition. Hamada initially visited Okinawa on his honeymoon, and often thereafter in the wintertime. The influence exerted by the Okinawa tradition may have been reinforced by his, no doubt, exhilarating romantic memory.

Fig. 163A. is a detail of Fig. 163.

H. 7 3/4 in. x diam. 4 in. (19.7 cm x 10.1 cm). S.J. & G.W. Lurie Collection.

Fig. 164. 1960s. A harmony of autumnal colors within a surface divided into four sections. Setting sunlight is the background for a single flower on a branch that slashes diagonally across. The rich persimmon glaze, bordered in green, is memorable.

H. 10 in. x w. 7 1/2 in. (25.4 x 19.05 cm). Private collection.

Fig. 165. 1960s. Hamada demonstrates his painting skill in using a pouring technique. Jackson Pollock-like, or perhaps Miro-like, this is an example of Hamada's interest in free abstraction, moving beyond his folk art roots.

Diam. 23 in. (58.4 cm). Private collection.

Koinuma Michio

(b. 1936)

Koinuma was born in Tokyo, where he studied politics and economics. At the age of 33, he moved to Mashiko and set up his own kiln. He still lives and works in Mashiko. His works are characterized by concrete-like clay, covered with fine gray ash deposits that give the impression that they have been excavated or produced in a Sue kiln. They are often strongly geometric or architectural with disciplined, controlled forms.

Fig. 166. c. 1990. A stripped-down, abstract walking figure. Grey kiln ash deposit reminds us of Japanese ceramic production going back to Sue ware. Clusters of design imply traditional clothing of some sort. The designs have been painted over the ash deposits, an open invitation for endless metaphorical interpretations, which, dear reader, will be resisted. An enlarged detail serves as the background for this piece.

H. 12 1/4 in. x w. 13 in. x d. 3 7/8 in. (31.1 cm x 33 cm x 9.8 cm). S.J. & G.W. Lurie Collection.

Fig. 166A. is a detail of Fig. 166.

Kamoda Shoji

(1933–1983)

Kamoda Shoji graduated art school where he studied under Tomimoto Kenkichi. His initial interest was to make natural wood ash glaze pieces inspired by ancient Sue ware. He moved to Mashiko for that purpose and achieved early success with this style. Success also brought many intrusive visitors. In 1969, Kamoda left Mashiko and set up a new kiln further north in the more isolated village of Tono, where, being a severe critic of his own work, he created new styles. Contrary to custom, he refused to attend his own exhibitions. Japanese ceramic connoisseurs have consistently rated his decorative work at the highest level. It was produced only for a period of about twenty years before his life was cut short by leukemia.

Fig. 167. *Painted Cylindrical Vase*, 1971; **Fig. 168.** *Jar With Pattern Of Waves*, 1970. Evocative shapes which strongly suggest, respectively, the body and hips of a high-breasted headless female, whose body is completely covered by tattoos or a dress; and the broad shoulders of a headless male torso. The female is decorated with a painted undulating red and white wave design; the male is wrapped in a raised wave pattern.

Fig. 167. H. 13.1 in. (33.2 cm). Private collection.

Fig. 168. H. 10.6 in. (27 cm). Hiroshima Prefectural Art Museum.

Fig. 169. *Painted Jar*, 1972. Kamoda Shoji became one of the finest decorative ceramic artists. A characteristic approach was to use wave-like bands of color, whose changing widths impart a feeling of motion as they wind around the vessel. In addition to the circular dots that outline and further animate the color bands, he orchestrated a handful of similar dots carefully placed over the surface as counterpoints. Kamoda had a great talent for making conventionally shaped pots exceptional.

H. 10.6 in. (27 cm). Private collection.

Matsui Kosei
(1927–2003)

Being a dedicated Buddhist head priest did not prevent Matsui from achieving the status of Living National Treasure for his ceramic art. He worked in Ibaraki Prefecture, close to Mishiko. He employed a special technique for making marbelized work. This involved tightly packing together layers of clay of various colors, then creatively cross-slicing through the clay sandwich at various angles to produce memorably colored and patterned vessels.

Fig. 170. In the work illustrated here, Matsui invokes Japanese blue and white textiles. This beautiful fragmented design calls to mind patchwork Buddhist robes intended to convey poverty and modesty. However, its exciting deep colors and odd sophisticated connected shapes dispel that interpretation. An ancestor, perhaps, is Ogata Kenzan's superb work illustrated in figure 46.

Private collection.

Ichigawa Kazuhiro

Fig. 171. c. 1999. The heavy influence of the great Chinese ceramic tradition is apparent in this work of the contemporary Kyushu artist, Ichigawa Kazuhiro. The front of the body and mouth have a black and silver oil drop glaze over a startling blue background. The rear body is pitch black. The disproportionate, soaring long neck is balanced by the small circular base with invaluable assistance from the two circular handles. The brown edging on the handles and rim are effective counterpoint details.

H. 10 $1/8$ in. x diam. 8 $1/4$ in. (25.7 cm x 20.9 cm). S.J. & G.W. Lurie Collection.

Tokuda Yasokichi
(b. 1933)

Tokuda Yasokichi's grandfather was celebrated for his work on Kutani pigments. Tokuda has retained the basic Kutani colors, but uses them only in their liveliest form. He did eliminate traditional Kutani designs, substituting ones that are less complicated but perfectly attuned to his brilliant colors. Tokuda Yasokichi was designated a Living National Treasure in 1997 for his innovations in Kutani pottery.

Fig. 172. 1999–2000. Tokuda has raised Kutani ware to a new level of excellence, with a modernist sensibility, best realized in his large plates which become his canvasses. The shape is, of course, completely traditional, except for its enormous size. But it makes no more sense to criticize the conventional shape of his large plates than it would be to criticize the conventional rectangular shape of a painter's canvass. He only works with porcelain and only uses traditional Kutani colors, chiefly deep blue, yellow, green and purple. Streams of these colors, sometimes pure, sometimes mixed with great finesse, pass from shade to shade. His designs include dramatic close-ups of flowers and blue-white flames, which intensify the visual experience. But, finally, it is color, color, color; overwhelming vibrant color that brings an appreciation of the near-mystical effects of color.

Diams up to 29 $1/2$ in. (74.9 cm). Private collections.

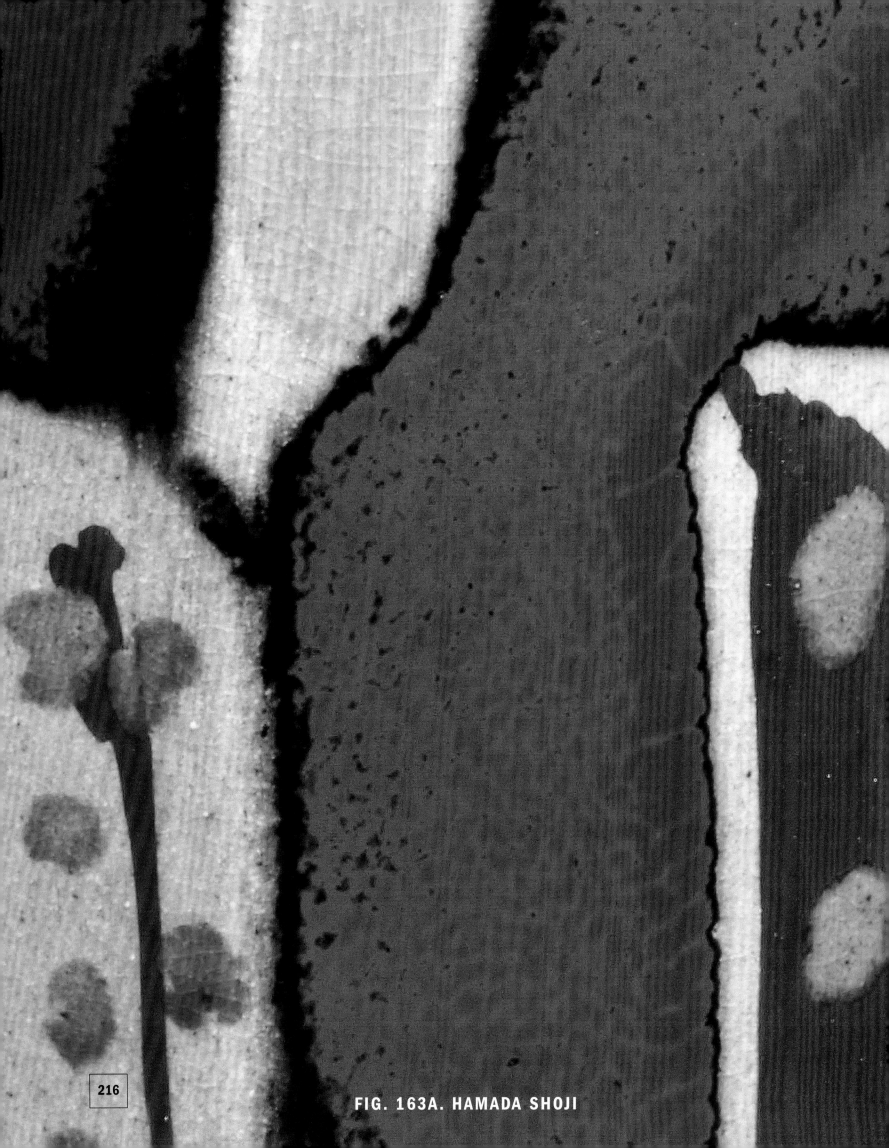

FIG. 163A. HAMADA SHOJI

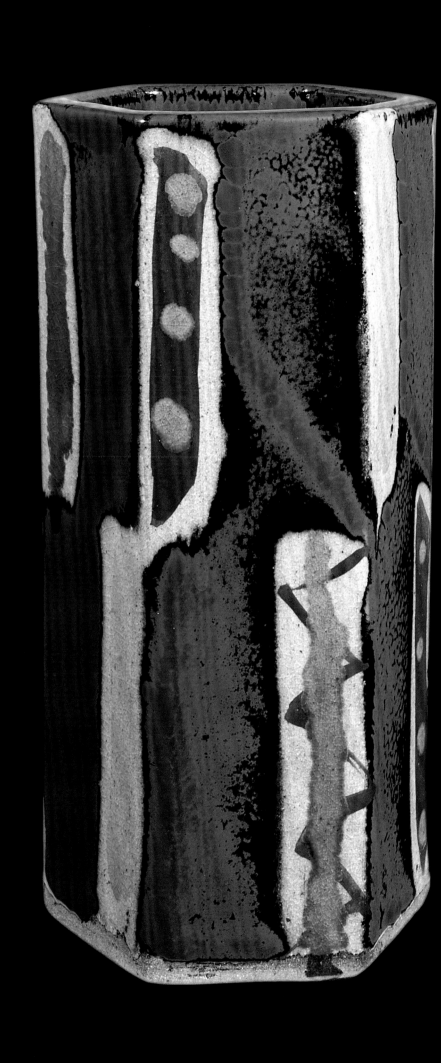

FIG. 163. HAMADA SHOJI

FIG. 164. HAMADA SHOJI

FIG. 165. HAMADA SHOJI

219

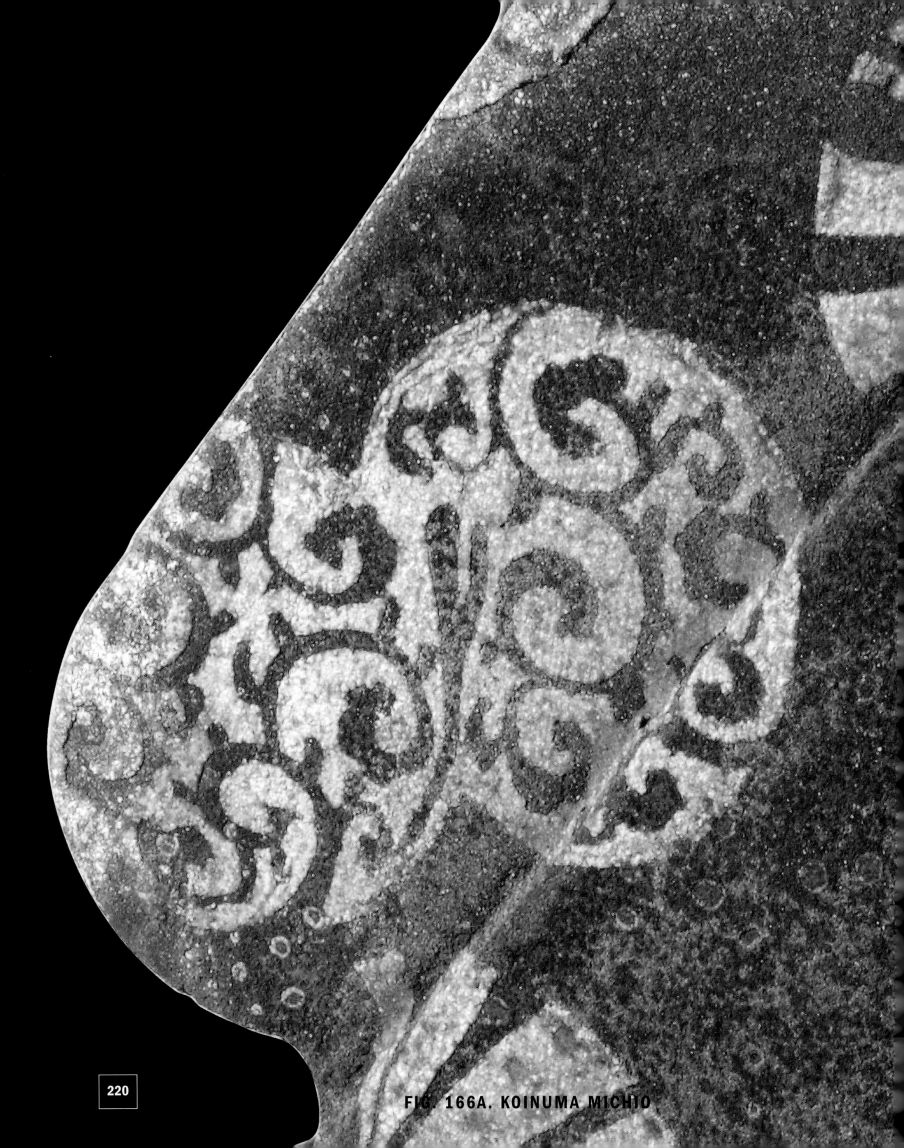

FIG. 166A. KOINUMA MICHIO

FIG. 166. KOINUMA MICHIO

221

FIGS. 167, 168. KAMODA SHOJI

FIG. 169. KAMODA SHOJI

223

FIG. 170. MATSUI KOSEI

FIG. 171. ICHIGAWA KAZUHIRO

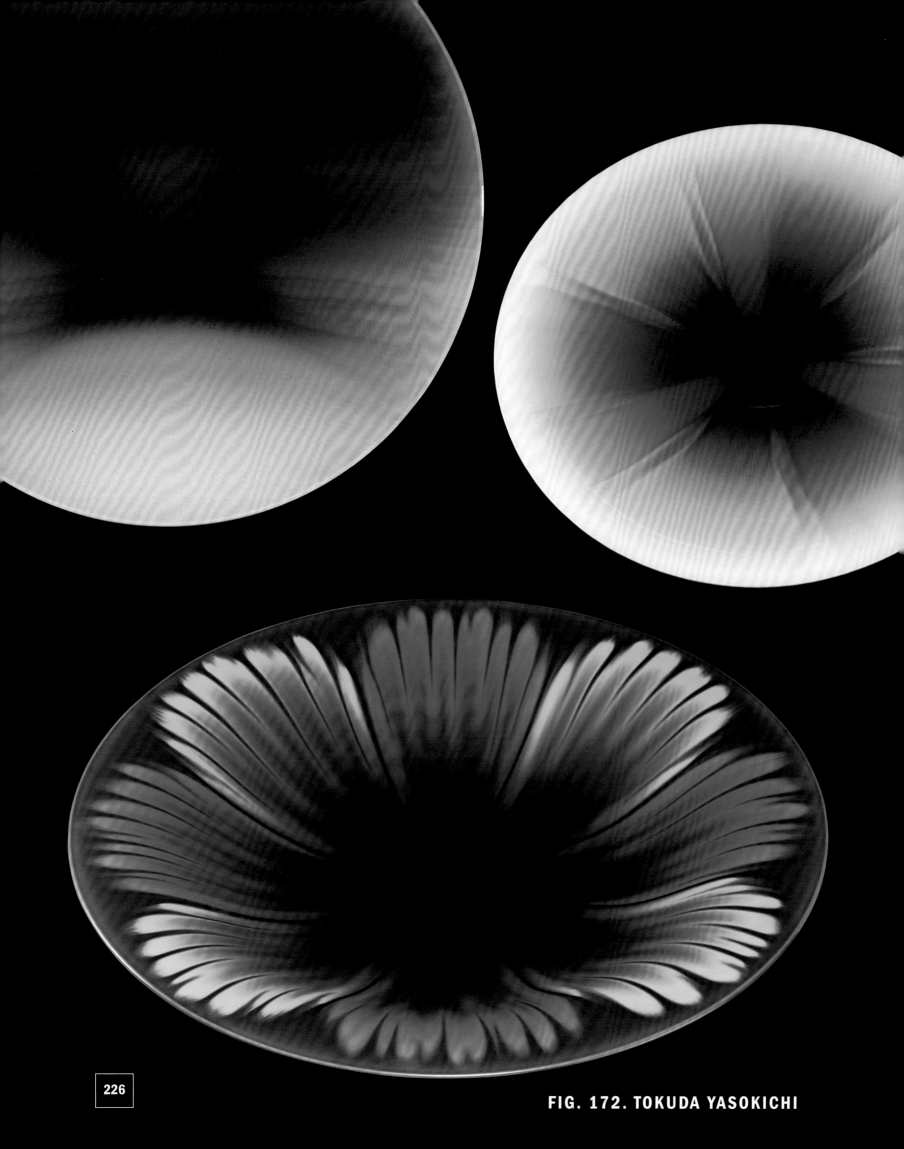

FIG. 172. TOKUDA YASOKICHI

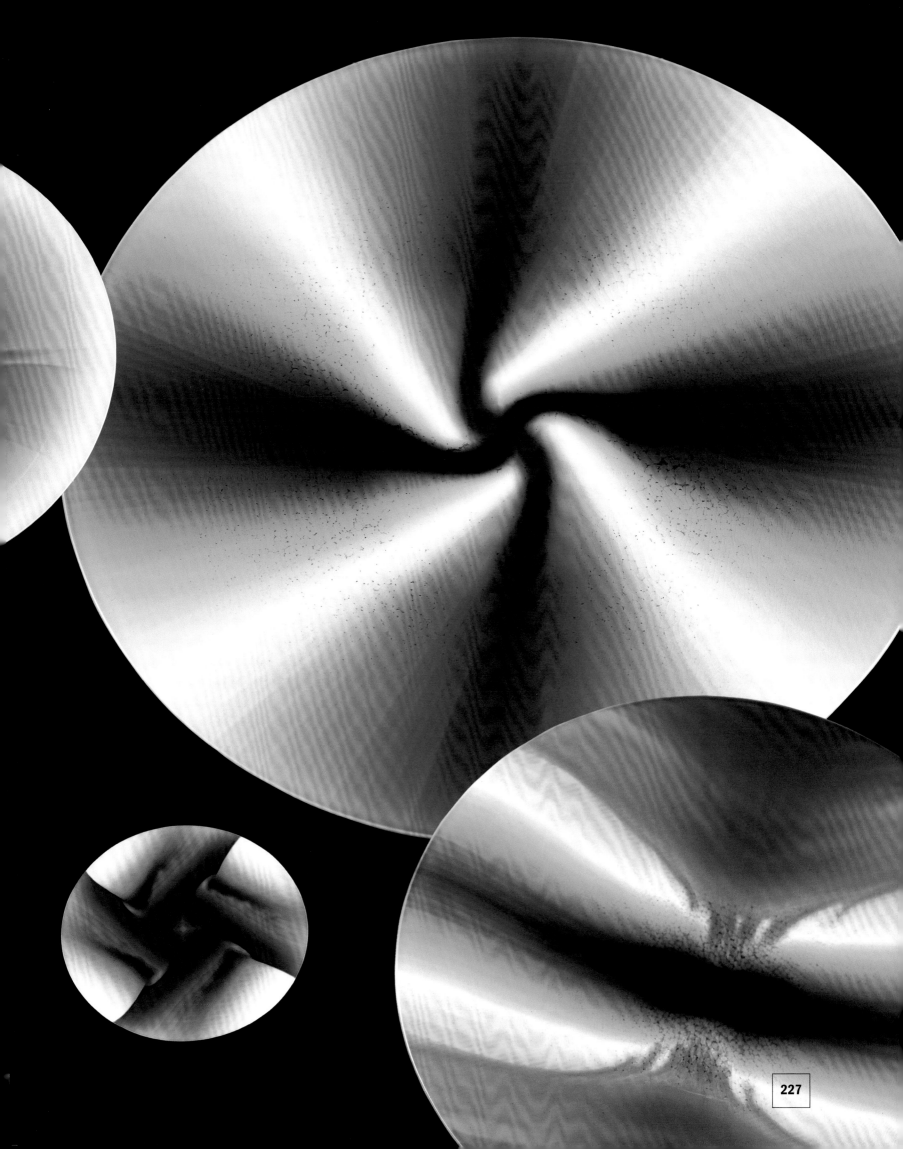

Tea Ceremony Bowls

Outside Japan, those without any prior knowledge of the tea ceremony are likely to be puzzled by the exalted significance of tea bowls in Japanese ceramics. The analogous beverage drink in the West is coffee, and there is no special aura of importance given to coffee cups. How can we understand this tea bowl phenomenon? A bit of history will prove useful.

The stimuli for some of the momentous changes in ceramic art can be traced back to the enthusiasm for the tea ceremony of the 15th century Shogun, Ashikaga Yoshimasa (1436–1490), which culminated in the 16th century when military leaders, Oda Nobunaga (1534–1582) and Toyotomi Hideyoshi (1536–1598), became tea practitioners. To this must be added the forcible importation into Japan of entire villages of Korean potters during the invasions of Korea by Hideyoshi in 1592 and 1597; the continuing influence of Sue ware aesthetics; the importance of Zen Buddhist practice; and the powerful leadership of a few remarkable tea masters, including Murata Juko (1422–1502), Takeno Joo (1502–1555), Sen-no Rikyu (1522–1591) and Furuta Oribe (1544–1615).

Green tea was first imported from China in the 8th century for medicinal use. Zen Buddhist monks drank green tea in order to remain awake during meditation. The drinking of tea and the rituals associated with preparing and serving it gradually evolved. At one point tea drinking was a boisterous affair practiced by the aristocracy and military lords. It was held in noisy large halls using expensive and showy utensils, chiefly from China. Murata Juko, the tea master for Shogun Ashikaga Yoshimasa, broke convention by insisting that the tea ceremony be per-formed in a simple, intimate room, in a calm atmosphere, with no alcohol consumption. He began the shift away from using luxurious, elegant Chinese utensils to simpler, unpretentious, inexpensive Japanese ware, such as Bizen and Shigaraki ware, to enhance the spiritual and aesthetic quality of the tea ceremony. Takeno Joo continued Juko's assessment that Bizen and Shigaraki ceramic tea ware possessed high aesthetic value, despite the fact, and partly because of the fact, that they had originally been made for ordinary daily use.

The next important figure was Sen-no Rikyu. Rikyu brought the tea ceremony to a state of perfection. He revered Juko's aesthetics, but preferred even greater austerity, verging on the appearance of poverty. Rikyu consolidated aesthetic values which we now regard as intrinsically Japanese. These include using the plainest utensils, a respect for seemingly artless ceramics that quietly and gradually reveal their beauty. Utensils which may contain kiln firing distortions and imperfections, previously considered undesirable, now were re-evaluated favorably as suggesting the withering effects of time and human limitations. Rikyu's tea room was an earthen-walled hut with a thatched roof, with all superfluous objects eliminated, austerely decorated with a single hanging scroll and/or flower vase. He preferred undecorated tea bowls, such as Korean rice bowls, as another means of expressing the rejection of material goods and emphasizing that true wealth is a matter of inner understanding. Rikyu recognized the appropriateness for his tea ceremony practice of ware that possessed the rustic beauty of natural wood ash glaze.

Rikyu was a tea master for the ruler Hideyoshi, who practiced the unaffected tea that Rikyu favored but, paradoxically, also practiced the vastly different tea in his famous golden teahouse whose interior was made of gold, including flower vases, water jars, tea bowls, walls, etc. It would seem that Hideyoshi, the son of a farmer who was also a part-time soldier, retained more than a vestige of nouveau-riche taste underneath the veneer of *wabi-sabi*, the unpretentious manner of performing the tea ceremony. In 1591, Hideyoshi turned against Rikyu for reasons now unknown, and ordered him to commit seppuku, ritual disembowelment. Rikyu composed two death poems, made tea for friends, and then committed ritual suicide.

We have already mentioned the importance of the introduction of higher-temperature Korean kilns in 5th-century Japan, which melted the wood ash. Sixteenth-century Momoyama pottery gloried in naturalism, embracing the naturally occurring wood ash deposited during the firing process. This prized pottery renounced all artificial glazes, all cosmetic alterations that would subvert and disguise its origin as the earth itself. Once its aesthetic value was accepted, what could be more satisfying than a wide range of richly colored and textured works of art produced solely from earth, fire, water and wood ash, the visual embodiment of a profound respect for the natural qualities of the materials?

Continuing the aesthetic revolt against perfectly made Chinese pottery and their immaculate glazed surfaces, Momoyama potters, and presumably their patrons and customers, valued what had been the unthinkable: certain deformations and cracks from kiln accidents. This should not be confused with tolerating poor craftsmanship. Momoyama potters were highly skilled and certainly would have destroyed all pots deformed in the kiln process had they considered these undesirable. On the contrary, their selective acceptance was determined by aesthetic criteria, reflecting the deep Japanese reverence

for all natural processes. Deformed pots became metaphors for the effects of the passage of time and mankind's limitations and imperfections. It was also linked to a philosophy of life which accepted the vicissitudes of life and recognized its essential uncertainty.

As we previously discussed, out of the general ferment of the Momoyama Period came a second innovative kind of pottery called Oribe (**figs. 10, 111–113**). Oribe ware can be seen as an abrupt, even more radical, rejection of traditional pottery values.

Rikyu's pupil, Furuta Oribe, had a very different approach to the tea ceremony. The name Oribe is attached to a large classification of ceramics, but his precise contribution to its creation is not known, although his encouragement and sponsorship were likely.

Furuta Oribe was a samurai, a tea advisor to the Shogun Tokugawa Ieyasu and, before that, had served as one of his generals. Oribe aesthetics represent a revolution against the tea utensils favored by Rikyu. Oribe ceramics strikingly depart, in every possible way, including form, color and pictorial design. Eccentric forms were deliberately made, rather than arising accidentally. Irregular, whimsical and asymmetrical shapes became a hallmark of Oribe tea ceremony utensils. Instead of muted or dark colors, Oribe ware features glazes of bright orange and green, dramatic contrasts of black and white, as well as painted decorations not found on earlier ceramics and largely drawn from textile designs, including geometric patterns, birds, flowers, plants and trees. All were unprecedented departures, an abrupt, radical attack on traditional pottery values. The effect was bold, gay and vitalizing. The solemnity and austerity of tea ceremony took hits on form, color and decoration.

Being a tea master is not thought of as a dangerous occupation, but Oribe's end was the same as Rikyu's. In 1615, Tokugawa Ieyasu ordered his death, for reasons now unknown. Oribe complied and committed ritual sui-cide. Quite obviously, the position of tea master to the Shogun was one of great authority and influence that car-ried commensurate risks.

Except for the artistic Shogun, Ashikaga Yoshimasa, it is hard to believe that spirituality or aesthetics was the primary motivation of the ruthless military leaders who embraced the tea ceremony. More likely, tea was a means of recognizing, strengthening and justifying their elite rank. We may speculate that, in their minds at least, the special knowledge of tea ceremony, available only to priv-ileged insiders, marked them as elevated connoisseurs worthy of the temporal power they exercised.

The innovations of Rikyu and Oribe reflect the creative power unleashed by a nation now unified and peaceful, enjoying the start of prosperity, and the self-confidence which it generated. Fundamental assumptions of ceramic art were questioned and overthrown. Rikyu's naturalism and Oribe's free spirit, two very different philosophies, both had revolutionary implications. Looking back to those Momoyama phenomena, we can see that within the tight political and social structure, some of Japan's cultural elite exhibited courageous artistic freedom. Explosive shifts in creative sensibility are not something that started in Europe 150 years ago, or in the USA during the 1950s. Momoyama Japan did it earlier. It is interesting to note that Oribe and Pop Art, and its progeny, share some similar core attitudes.

Since the late 16th century, tea bowls have been among the most expensive ceramic vessels. Even today, before a serious ceramic artist will make a tea bowl, the artist must feel that he or she has enough wisdom and experience to perform this near-sacred act. Each tea bowl is connected to the otherworldly spirit of the tea ceremony. Japanese ceramists are keenly aware that, in making a tea bowl, they are following a long and great tradition of earlier artists, who had fulfilled this function honorably,

with sincerity and sensitivity. Many of the most celebrated ceramic sculptors of the last sixty years take a special pride in making a limited number of tea bowls. To them, the importance of a great tea bowl overrides every consid-eration of contemporary art theory and art preferences. The tea bowl tradition is a continuing legacy of the essence of Japanese culture.

Tea bowls are meant to be actually used to drink tea from, and the illustrated tea bowls were undoubtedly designed for use in the tea ceremony. Evaluation of tea bowls is radically different from the evaluation of all other ceramics. To fully appreciate and properly evaluate tea bowls, they must be sensitively held in the hands, slowly turned (**Fig. 173**). The weight and balance of the bowl, its texture, contours and shape should be savored by the hands and lips as much as by the eyes. The surface design, often of great subtlety and abstraction, and the degree of slope of the interior wall, require enough time for dedicated viewing.

Lips must address the rim, voluptuous or creamy, perhaps roughened or bumpy, thin or thick, irregular in an unpredictable way or, yes, uneventfully commonplace. This oral element provides a unique dimension in art connoisseurship.

When the tea is actually being drunk, the sensation of taste is added, along with the impact of the color of frothy green tea against the color of the interior of the bowl. Tea ceremony is a social occasion with complex interpersonal interactions, especially since it often takes place in a spe-cially designed tea room with a distinctive minimalist ambiance. That tea room may be accessed only through a very low entryway, forcing everyone to crawl inside on their hands and knees. The room itself may be extremely small, forcing participants to sit close together. An atmosphere of humility and human equality, regardless of rank, wealth, beauty, age or celebrity, is created. This is furthered by the requirement that all jewelry must be removed before entering the tea room. In the tea room at least, Imperial Japan from the Momoyama Period onward invented a vehicle to express the ideal of equality as perfectly as any Western practice.

It is not easy to understand the power of complex, simultaneous tactile, visual and taste sensations, primitive sensory stimuli complicated by intimate, perhaps novel, personal relationships within the special conditions of the tea room. All these factors somehow combine and interact to produce the spiritual and other higher experiences of tea ceremony.

During the tea ceremony, participants will carefully examine the tea bowls and may express their views as to their aesthetic properties. This deliberate, close consideration of a small object, one that might ordinarily be casually used as a utilitarian vessel, can be extrapolated to provide a valuable insight. We all have the potential to see unexpected beauty in the numberless places, events and things, large and small, of our everyday existence.

Nine of the fourteen bowls illustrated are in museums and unavailable for handling and actual use. There was little choice except to select those ancient tea bowls solely on the basis of visual observation of the bowl and/or by a photograph. Even without proper access, which limits understanding, these tea bowls clearly show great merit.

Fig. 173. An illustration of a moment in the tea ceremony, when the tea bowl is being sensitively held in both hands.
Figs. 174, 175, 176. Momoyama Period (1568–1603). These three tea bowls, Shino (fig. 174), Black Oribe (fig. 175), and Oribe (fig. 176), declare their independence from previously ascendent Chinese models. They depart in form: square and shallow (figs. 175, 176); cylindrical with no visible foot (fig. 174). They depart in decoration by their extensive use of abstractions: vibrantly painted distorted wheel shapes on a tea bowl known as Yamaji (fig. 176); sketched parallel lines suggesting a deserted bridge amidst a snowy field (fig. 174); white triangles and circles suggesting trees, perhaps triangular shaped pine trees, and fruit or flowers (fig. 175). They declare unprecedented aesthetic interests: irreverent pop gaiety (fig. 176); winter's barrenness (fig. 174); basic geometric forms (fig. 175).

Fig. 174. H. 4 1/2 in. (11.4 cm). Tokyo National Museum.

Fig. 175. H. 3 in. x 5 3/4 in. x 4 in. (7.6 cm. x 14.6 cm x 10 cm). Private collection.

Fig. 176. H. 2 1/2 in. (6.4 cm). Private collection.

Fig. 177. Ogata Kenzan, 17th–18th century. Edo Period (1603–1868). This tea bowl is a masterpiece, seemingly a rapidly painted, artless impression of early spring. The dramatic black tree limb is adjacent to red and white flowers and green grass, making a fragrant bouquet. The old tree limb has given life to young, vibrant flowers. Not until some 100 years later were artists in the West painting in such a loose, summary, yet convincing style.

Diam. 4 in. (10.1 cm). Private collection.

Fig. 178. Nonomura Ninsei,17th century. Edo Period (1603–1868). A return to a more conventionally formed tea bowl: level rim, well-crafted symmetrical sides, resting on a visible foot. Ninsei provides an elegant and exquisite interplay between cresting waves and a sea level view of the crescent moon. Only a few decades after the Momoyama Period, we find this new aesthetic prevailing, much more easygoing and readily likeable. The emergence of the merchant class, now becoming prosperous, as tastemakers, was an important factor in this change.

H. 4 in. x diam. 5 in. (10.1 cm x 12.7 cm). Tokyo National Museum.

Fig. 179. Wakao Toshisada, 2002. Wakao's deeply-felt message is: like the camellias that blossom in the winter, life can be beautiful even during a time of hardship. While giving us present delight, this tea bowl remembers its roots in Shino tradition. The wonderfully depicted flowers, set on a bluish field, resonate with soul.

H. 4 3/16 in. x d. 5 1/2 in. (10.6 cm x 13.9 cm). Private collection.

Fig. 180. Arakawa Toyozo, 1957. Arakawa's homage to Momoyama Shino ware. A tea bowl with a chilling reminder of winter's frigidity. The thick white crackled glaze can be seen as a field of snow. The frosty cold has driven all the leaves from the few surviving blackened branches of the tree, surrounded by an endless snow field. This may also be read as a reflection on a lingering dispirited mood or other bleak feelings.

H. 3 1/2 in. x diam. 5 in. (8.9 cm x 12.7 cm). Tokyo National Museum.

Fig. 181. Kato Tsubusa, 2002. Kato deconstructs the long-accepted concept of porcelain ware. His porcelain tea bowl lacks the appearance of perfect craftsmanship, disappoints expected elegance, and brandishes what superficially appears to be unfinished, careless workmanship. Some areas are unglazed, the sides irregular, the glaze pools randomly located. More careful observation shows, instead, a brilliantly original and satisfying composition. Each previously disturbing element, quite simply, works and is fresher for having combined unlikely elements. His flowing celadon glaze is a dynamic, rather than a still beauty. Imagine how fresh foamy green tea would look against the virginal interior. Of substantial weight, its smooth surface contrasts nicely with the irregularly-spaced, sharply-faceted vertical edges, yet manages to fit comfortably in one's hands. Despite its differences from traditional celadon work, it retains the ethereal celadon silent beauty.

H. 4 3/4 in. x diam. 5 1/2 in. (12 cm x 14 cm). S.J. & G.W. Lurie Collection.

Fig. 182. Suzuki Osamu (b. 1934), 2002. He is not the earlier Sodeisha Suzuki Osamu. Suzuki continues the Shino tradition, but the white glaze is no longer an overall covering. It has been dramatically segmented into strong interlocking white sections. Its lip is inviting, curvy and crossed at intervals by a creamy white glaze.

H. 4 in. x diam. 5 1/2 in. (10.1 cm x 14 cm). Museum of Modern Ceramic Art, Gifu.

Fig. 183. Kato Takahiro (b. 1972), 2004. A younger potter continuing a distinguished family tradition. This large tea bowl is as exciting to look at as it is to hold in one's hands. The raised white Shino glaze runs in slashing diagonal paths over unglazed dry clay; the rim rises and falls unpredictably. This tea bowl protests the regulated movements of the tea ceremony and its traditional staid ambiance. It prefers improvisation, spontaneity, movement and surprise.

H. 4 3/8 in. x diam. 5 1/4 in. (11.1 cm x 13.3 cm). S.J. & G.W. Lurie Collection.

Fig. 184. Kaneshige Toyo, c. 1960. Its restrained luminosity facilitates serene enlightenment, one of the rewards of tea practice. Generously proportioned, it employs understatement and disciplined control. Also illustrated on p. xvii.

Fig. 185. Raku Kichizaemon XV (b. 1949), 1999. He studied art in Europe and brought an international sensibility to his 400-year family pottery-making legacy. This tea bowl was coiled and carved, and is topped with a challenging craggy rim. Its thoughtfully subdued colored surface has a mystic aura, conducive to contemplation.

H. 4 3/4 in. x 5 1/2 in. (12 cm x 14 cm). Museum of Modern Ceramic Art, Gifu.

H. 2.9 in. x d. 5.5 in. (7.3 cm x 14 cm); Toyo Kaneshige Kinenkan.

Fig. 186. Matsuda Yuriko, 2001. The tea ceremony has been turned into a technicolor celebration. The meditative is submerged by strips of playful, merrily colored designs. Matsuda unconventionally built this tea bowl by laying strips of clay over a mold. Although far different in appearance, it embodies the rebellious happy spirit of Momoyama Oribe work. Cheers to life!

H. 3 1/2 in. x diam. 4 in. (8.9 cm. x 10.1 cm). S.J. & G.W. Lurie Collection.

Fig. 187. Kohara Yasuhiro, 2003. A contemporary variation on traditional natural wood ash glaze pottery. His distinctive green jewel-like fused drops of wood ash glaze provide a dramatic focus. The surface is alternately gritty and slick-smooth from running glaze, vivid reminders of its fiery birth.

H. 3 1/2 in. x diam. 5 1/2 in. (8.9 cm x 14 cm). S.J. & G.W. Lurie Collection.

FIG. 173.

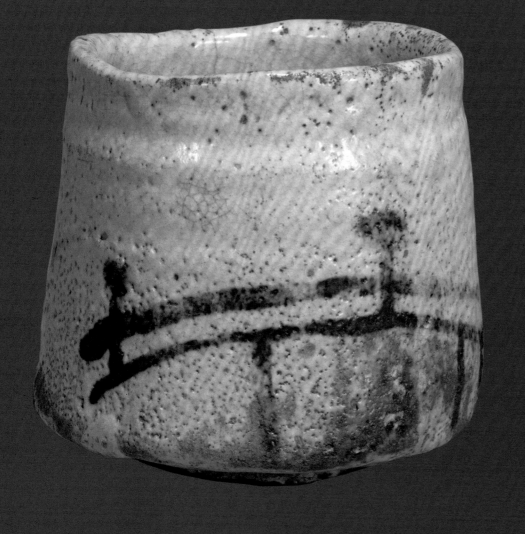

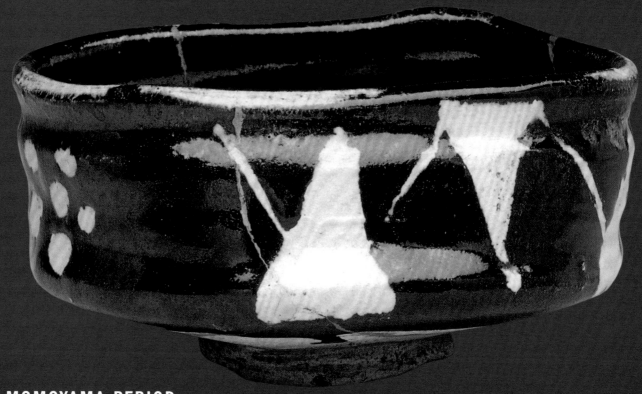

MOMOYAMA PERIOD
FIG. 174. SHINO TEA BOWL.
FIG. 175. BLACK ORIBE TEA BOWL.

MOMOYAMA PERIOD
FIG. 176. ORIBE TEA BOWL

235

FIG. 177. OGATA KENZAN

FIG. 178.
NONOMURA NINSEI
FIG. 179. WAKAO TOSHISADA

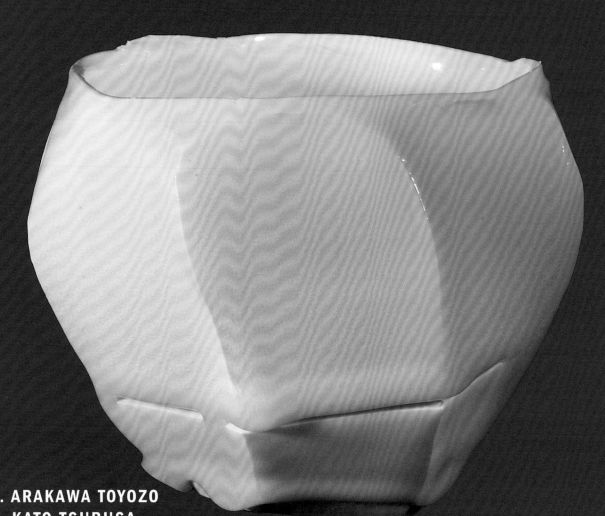

FIG. 180. ARAKAWA TOYOZO
FIG. 181. KATO TSUBUSA

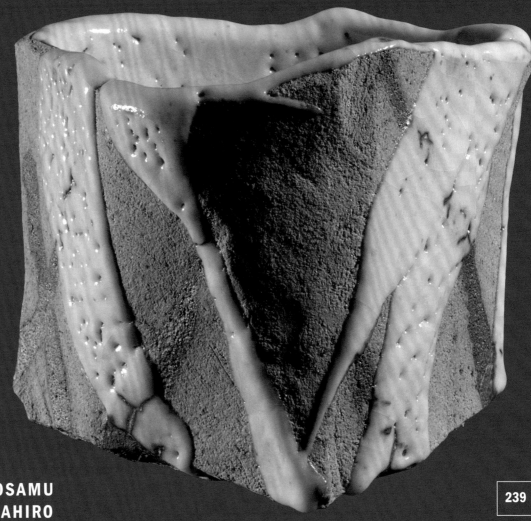

FIG. 182. SUZUKI OSAMU
FIG. 183. KATO TAKAHIRO

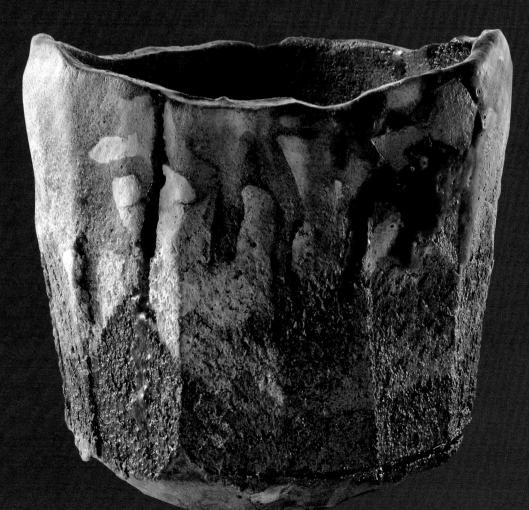

FIG. 184. KANESHIGE TOYO
FIG. 185. RAKU KICHIZAEMON

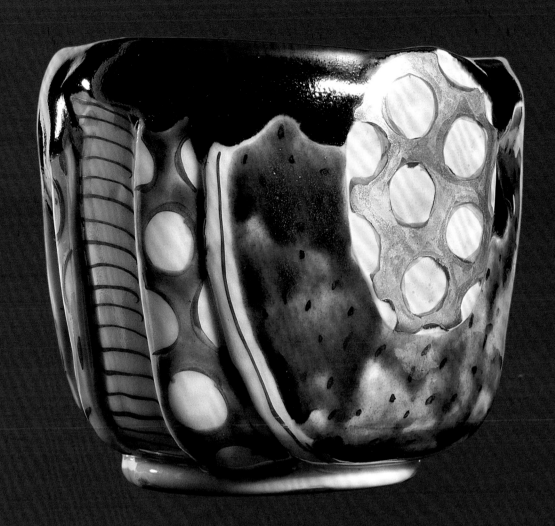

FIG. 186. MATSUDA YURIKO
FIG. 187. KOHARA YASUHIRO

Further Reading

Aichi Prefectural Ceramic Museum. *The Development of Japanese Ceramics.* Aichi: Aichi Prefectural Ceramic Museum, 2002.

——. *Current Trends in Ceramics: Vessels and Objects,* 1994.

Art Complex Museum. *Shaped with a Passion: The Carl A. Weyerhaeuser Collection of Japanese Ceramics from the 1970s.* Duxbury, MA: Art Complex Museum, 1998.

Baekeland, Frederick and Robert Mose. *Modern Japanese Ceramics in American Collections.* New York: Japan Society, 1993.

Berenson, Bernard. *The Italian Painters of the Renaissance.* London and New York: Phaidon, 1952.

Cardozo, Sidney B. *The Art of Rosanjin.* Tokyo: Kodansha, 1987.

——. *The Ceramic Art of Kitaoji Rosanjin.* Tokyo: Benrido, 1964.

Cort, Louise Allison. *Shigaraki: Potter's Valley.* New York: Weatherhill, 1979.

——. *Isamu Noguchi and Modern Japanese Ceramics.* Washington, D.C.: The Arthur M. Sackler Gallery, Smithsonian Institution, 2003.

——. and Shinya Maezaki. *Genesis of a Genius: The Early Ceramics of Fukami Sueharu.* Hanford, CA: The Ruth & Sherman Lee Institute for Japanese Art at the Clark Center, 2003.

Egami, Namio. *The Beginnings of Japanese Art.* New York /Tokyo: Weatherhill/Heibonsha, 1973.

Faulkner, Rupert. *Japanese Studio Crafts: Tradition and the Avant-Garde.* London: Laurence King Publishing, 1995.

Fujioka, Ryoichi. *Shino and Oribe Ceramics.* Japanese Arts Library, vol. 1. Tokyo: Kodansha, 1977.

Gifu Ceramic Museum. *Karatsu, Iga & Bizen in the Momoyama-Mino Area.* Gifu: Gifu Ceramic Museum, 2003.

Gunma Prefecture Museum of History. *Haniwa.* Gunma: Gunma Prefecture Museum of History, 1996.

Hayashi, Seizo. *Momoyama Period II: Mino Ware, Chojiro and Koetsu.* Ceramic Art of the World, vol. 5. Tokyo: Shogakukan, 1976.

Hayashi, Yasuo. *Chronology and Related Materials.* Kyoto: Hayashi Yasuo, 1987.

——. *The Works of Yasuo Hayashi.* Tokyo: Kawado Shodo Shinsha, 1998.

Ibaraki Ceramics Museum. *White Porcelain and Celadon: Itaya Hazan, Tomimoto Kenkichi.* Ibaraki: Ibaraki Ceramics Museum, 2003.

Idemitsu Museum of Art. *Hazan Itaya.* Tokyo: Idemitsu Museum of Art, 1994.

Imamura, Keiji. *Prehistoric Japan: New Perspectives on Insular East Asia.* Honolulu: University of Hawaii Press, 1966.

Inui, Yoshiaki. *Shoji Hamada. Contemporary Japanese Ceramics,* vol. 7. Tokyo: Shueisha, 1981.

——. *Yagi Kazuo. A Pageant of Modern Japanese Ceramics,* vol. 14. Shusheisha, 1982.

——. *Kanjiro Kawai. Contemporary Japanese Ceramics,* vol. 4. Tokyo: Shueisha, 1980.

—— *Kazuo Yagi. Contemporary Japanese Ceramics,* vol. 14. Tokyo: Shueisha, 1982.

Japan Society, New York. *The Rise of a Great Tradition: Japanese Archaeological Ceramics From the Jomon Through Heian Periods (10,500 BC–AD 1185).* New York: Japan Society, 1990.

Kanoh Museum. *Toyo Kaneshige.* Kanoh Museum, 1997.

Kawahara, Masahiko. *The Ceramic Art of Ogata Kenzan.* Japanese Arts Library, vol. 13. Tokyo: Kodansha, 1985.

Kidder, J. Edward. *The Birth of Japanese Art.* New York: Frederick A. Praeger, 1965.

——. *Prehistoric Japanese Arts: Jomon Pottery.* Tokyo: Kodansha, 1968.

Kobayashi, Tatsuo. *Jomon Pottery. Archaeological Treasures of Japan,* vol. 1. Tokyo: Kodansha, 1977.

——. *Jomon Reflections: Forager Life and Culture in the Prehistoric Japanese Archipelago.* Oxbow Books, 2004

Kobayashi, Yukio. *Haniwa. Survey of Ceramics,* vol. 3. Tokyo: Heibonsha, 1974.

——. *Jomon. Survey of Ceramics,* vol. 1. Tokyo: Heibonsha, 1990.

Kyoto Shoin. *The Best Selection of Contemporary Ceramics in Japan.* Kyoto: Kyoto Shoin (various years).

——. *Toshisada Wakao,* Toh vol. 20, 1992;

——. *Yuriko Matsuda,* Toh vol. 34, 1992;

——. *Zenji Miyashita,* Toh vol. 37, 1992;

——. *Kosuke Kaneshige.* Toh vol. 45, 1992;

——. *Takiguchi Kazuo*, Toh vol. 53, 1992;

——. *Anjin Abe*, Toh vol. 61, 1993;

——. *Taimei Morino*, Toh vol. 65, 1993;

——. *Tsubusa Kato*, Toh vol. 85, 1993.

——. *Rikichi Miyanaga*, Toh vol. 64, 1993.

Leach, Bernard. *Hamada: Potter*. Kodansha International, Ltd., 1975.

Masahiko, Kawahara. *Ceramic Art of Ogata Kenzan*. Kodansha: 1985.

Mashiko Ceramics Museum. *Kamoda Shoji*. Inshosha, 2004.

Miho Museum. *Complete Works of Shigaraki Old Jars*. Tokyo: Shogakukan, 1999.

——. *Ko-Shigaraki: Jars from Shigaraki's Medieval Kilns*. Shigaraki: Miho Museum, 1999.

Mikaki, Tsugio. *The Art of Japanese Ceramics*. New York/Tokyo: Weatherhill/Heibonsha, 1972.

Miller, Roy Andrew. *Japanese Ceramics*. Toto Shuppa, 1960.

Mitsuoka, Tadanori, Naoshige Okuda. *Momoyama Period I: Bizen, Tamba, Shigaraki and Iga Wares*. Ceramic Art of the World, vol. 4. Tokyo: Shogakukan, 1977.

Moes, Robert. *Japanese Ceramics*. New York: The Brooklyn Museum, 1979.

Murase, Miyeko, ed. *Turning Point: Oribe and the Arts of Sixteenth-Century Japan*. New York: The Metropolitan Museum of Art, 2003

Musee Tomo. *Japanese Ceramics Today, Part 1: Masterworks from the Kikuchi Collection*. Tokyo: Musee Tomo, 2003.

The Museum of Art, Kochi. *Modern Ceramics and 14 Pioneers*. Kochi: The Museum of Art, 2003.

Museum of Modern Ceramic Art, Gifu. *The Legacy of Modern Ceramic Art, Part 1: From Artisan to Artists, the Evolution of Japanese Ceramic Art*. Gifu: Museum of Modern Ceramic Art, 2002.

Nagamine, Mitsukazu and Masayoshi Mizuno. *Clay Figures, Haniwa*. Archaeological Treasures of Japan, vol.3. Tokyo: Kodansha, 1977.

Nakanishi, Toru. *Old Tamba*. Tokyo: Bijutsukan, 1978.

——. *Japanese Medieval Period*. Art of the World, vol. 3. Tokyo: Shogakukan, 1977.

Narasaki, Shoichi. *Japanese Ancient Period*. Ceramic Art of the World, vol. 2. Tokyo: Shogakukan, 1979

The National Museum of Modern Art, Tokyo. *The Retrospective Exhibition of Shoji Hamada*. Tokyo: Nihon Keizai Shimbun, 1977.

——. *Kawai Kanjiro: Master of Modern Japanese Ceramics*. Tokyo: Nihon Keizai Shimbun, 1984.

——. Kamoda Shoji: *A Prominent Figure in Contemporary Ceramics*. Tokyo: Nihon Keizai Shimbun, 1987.

——. *Ceramic Art of Suzuki Osamu: Poetry in Ceramic Works*. Tokyo: Nihon Keizai Shimbun, 1999.

——. *Modern Revival of Momoyama Ceramics: Turning Point Toward Modernization of Ceramics*. Tokyo: Nihon Keizai Shimbun, 2002.

The National Museum of Modern Art, Kyoto. *Kazuo Yagi Exhibition*. Tokyo: Nihon Keizai Shimbun, 1981.

——. *Exhibition of Kanjiro Kawai*, Kyoto: The National Museum of Modern Art, 1983.

——. *Crafts in Kyoto [1945-2000]*. 2001.

Nezu Institute of Fine Arts. *Catalogue of Selected Masterpieces from the Nezu Collections: Decorative Art*. Nezu: Nezu Institute of Fine Arts, 2001.

Nihon Keizai Shimbun. *Shoji Kamoda Ceramic Exhibition*. Tokyo: Nihon Keizai Shimbun, 1980.

Okada, Jo. *Toyozo Arakawa*. Living National Treasures Series, vol. 1. Tokyo: Kodansha, 1977.

Okada, Soei. *All about Ko Bizen*. Tokyo: Shojusha Bijutsu Shuppan, 1988.

Sanders, Herbert H. *The World of Japanese Ceramics*. Tokyo: Kodansha, 1982.

Sano Museum. *Kitaoji Rosanjin*. Sano Museum, 2003.

Sanyo Shimbun. *Living National Treasure: Kei Fujiwara Retrospective Exhibition*. Okayama: Sanyo Shimbun, 1984.

Shigaraki Ceramic Cultural Park. *Great Shigaraki Exhibition: Rediscovery & Revival of the Beauty of Yakishime Stoneware*, 2001.

——. *The Heart of the Creator in Contemporary Ceramic Art*. 1998.

Shimizu, Masako and Yukihiko Ishii. *Creative Tradition: The Ceramics of Rosanjin and Masterpieces of the Past Which Influenced Him*. Tokyo: Setagaya Art Museun, 1996.

Sugihara, Shosuke. *Yayoi Vessels*. Japanese Primitive Art, vol. 3. Tokyo: Kodansha, 1964.

Suntory Museum. *Japanese Ceramics 1200 Years: from Nara Sansai to Imari, Nabeshima, Ninsei and Kanzan*. Tokyo: Suntory Museum, 2003.

Suzuki, Tsutomu. *Ceramic Art from National Treasures & Important Cultural Properties*. Tokyo: Sekai Bunka-sha, 1978.

Takakura, Hiroaki. *Yayoi*. Tokyo: Kobunsha, 1992.

Takeuchi, Hiroshi. *Jomon Clay Figurines*. Tokyo: Kinokuniya, 1959

Takeuchi, Junichi. *Oribe*. Complete Works of Japanese Ceramics, vol. 16. Tokyo: Chuo Koron-sha, 1976.

Tamba Museum. *The Best of Ko-Tamba Works*. Tamba: Tamba Museum, 1989

Tanabe, Shozo. *Yayoi & Haji*. Survey of Japanese Ceramics, vol. 2. Tokyo: Heibonsha, 1978.

——. *Sue*. Survey of Japanese Ceramics, vol. 4. Tokyo: Heibonsha, 1989.

Toda, Tetsuya. *Jomon.* Tokyo: Kobunsha, 1991.

Todate, Kazuko. *The Captivation Of Bizen Ware Non-Glazed Stoneware*. Ibaraki: Ibaraki Ceramics Museum, 2004

——. *The Quintessence of Modern Japanese Ceramics*, Ibaraki Ceramics Museum, 2006.

Toguri Museum. *Selected Works from Toguri Museum Collection*. Tokyo: Toguri Museum, 2000.

Tokuda, Yasokichi. *The Works of Yasokichi Tokuda*. Tokyo: Kodansha, 1995.

Tokyo National Museum. *Clay Objects of Ancient Japan: From Jomon and Yayoi periods*. Tokyo National Museum, 2001.

Tsuboi, Kiyotari. *Japanese Prehistoric Period*. Ceramic Art of the World, vol. 1. Tokyo: Shogakukan, 1979.

——. *Yayoi*. Survey of Japanese Ceramics, vol. 2. Tokyo: Heibonsha, 1990. Sato Masahiko. *Tokyo Ceramics*. New York/Tokyo: Weatherhill/Shibundo , 1973.

Wilson, Richard L. *The Art of Ogata Kenzan: Persona and Production in Japanese Ceramics*. New York: Weatherhill, 1991.

——. *Potter's Brush: the Kenzan Style in Japanese Ceramics*. Washington D.C.: Freer Gallery of Art and Arthur M. Sackler Gallery, Smithsonian Institution, 2001.

World Ceramic Festival Committee. *"Primitivism" in Contemporary Ceramics*. Shigaraki: World Ceramic Festival Committee, 1990.

Yabe, Yoshiaki. *Nabeshima*. Complete Works of Japanese Ceramics, vol. 25. Tokyo: Chuo Koronsha, 1976.

Yanagi, Soetsu. *The Unknown Craftsman*. Tokyo, New York, and San Francisco: Kodansha International, 1972.

Yoshida, Kozo, ed. *Kei Fujiwara*. Japanese Ceramics: Contemporary Masters, vol. 13. Tokyo: Kodansha, 1977.

——, *Toyozo Arakawa*. Contemporary Japanese Ceramics, vol. 6. Tokyo: Shueisha, 1981.

Photography Credits

All photographs are credited—**by figure number**—to Geoff Spear, except as noted.

Aichi Prefectural Ceramic Museum 142, 161

Alexandra Nogoita 56, 58, 98, 99, 100, 101, 103, 120, 121, 123, 179

Ezaki Yoshikazu 169

Fukuoka Art Museum, Matusnaga Collection 45

Goto Kiyoshi 79, 80, 81

Gregory R. Staley 51, 219

Haruka Tsukada, Gallery Mukyo 152

Hatakeyama Memorial Museum of Fine Art 9

Hatakeyama Takashi 9, 60, 60A, 61, 62, 71, 75, 76, 77, 78

Hiroshima Prefectural Museum 31, 168

Ibaraki Ceramics Museum 79

Idemitsu Museum of Arts 18, 20

Inui Tsuyoshi 167

Itsuo Art Museum 46A

John Bigelow Taylor 107, 117

Kawai Kanjiro's House 52, 54

Kitamura Museum 113

Kiyoshikojin Seicho-ji Temple 130

Kobayashi Yoji p. xvi, 95

Kyoto Municipal Museum of Art 23, 29

Kyushu Historical Museum 8

Misho-ryu Nakayama Bunpokai 21

MOA Museum of Art 12

Museum of Modern Art, Kamakura & Hayama 32

Museum of Modern Ceramic Art, Gifu 19, 42, 43, 182, 185

Nagaoka Municipal Science Museum 1

Nakamura Akio 89, 90

National Museum of Modern Art, Kyoto 44, 46, 49, 53, 55

Private Collection 22, 28, 33, 34, 35, 37, 38, 40, 47, 47A, 59, 109, 122, 134, 135, 137, 141, 148, 149, 150, 151, 157, 170, 172, 175, 176, 177

Saiki Taku 144, 146

Setagaya Museum of Art 153, 154

Shigaraki Ceramic Culture Park 39, 41, 81

Suntory Museum of Art 14, 111, 112, 128

Toyo Kaneshige Kinenkan 87, 88, 184

Tokyo National Museum 3, 4, 6, 7, 13, 15, 16, 17, 48, 84, 127, 174, 178, 180

Tokyo National Museum of Modern Art 80, 86

Toyozo Museum 129, 131

Yamanashi Prefectural Museum of Archaeology 2